No Boundaries

No Boundaries

A Cancer Surgeon's Odyssey

LaSalle D. Leffall Jr., M.D.

Howard University Press
Washington, D.C. 20059

Howard University Press, Washington, D.C. 20059

Copyright © 2005 by LaSalle D. Leffall Jr.
All rights reserved.

WWW.HUPRESS.HOWARD.EDU

LIBRARY OF CONGRESS CATALOGING-IN-PUBLICATION DATA

Leffall, LaSalle D.
  No boundaries : a cancer surgeon's odyssey / by Lasalle D. Leffall, Jr.
    p. cm.
  Includes bibliographical references and index.
  ISBN 0-88258-251-8 (978-0-88258-251-1 : alk. paper)
  1. Leffall, LaSalle D. 2. Oncologists—Washington (D.C.)—Biography.
I. Title.
  RC279.6.L44A3 2005
  616.99'4'0092—dc22

                                                        2005020998

The author wishes to thank Dr. K. Jill Odeku for her kind permission to reprint the poem, "Learning to Expect," from her late husband Dr. E. Latunde Odeku's 1964 collection, "Twilight Out of the Night."

Text and Cover Design by Sans Serif, Inc.

Manufactured in the United States of America
This book is printed on acid-free paper.

10 9 8 7 6 5 4 3 2 1

To Ruthie and Donney

"Surgery, after all, is an affair of the spirit, it is a fierce test of a man's technical skill, sometimes, but in a grim or long fight, it is above all a trial of the spirit: and there are few things that cannot be conquered if a man's heart is set on victory."

SIR BERKELEY MOYNIHAN
(Letter to Dr. Charles M. Graney)

CONTENTS

FOREWORD

John R. Seffrin, Ph.D.
Chief Executive Officer
American Cancer Society

If this book conveys nothing else, it brilliantly illustrates the possibilities of challenging the status quo. For LaSalle Leffall, who grew up in the Depression-era South, the status quo was shaped by stifling Jim Crow laws, discrimination, and segregation. However, these barriers neither confined nor defined LaSalle's dreams for success. Throughout his memoirs you will see how LaSalle took to heart and lived the advice given to him by his mentor, Charles R. Drew, a former Howard University College of Medicine chief of surgery: "Excellence of performance will transcend artificial barriers created by man." Indeed, LaSalle's is a fascinating and inspirational life marked by a powerful drive to succeed in spite of daunting challenges, an invaluable gift for the practice of medicine, and a profound desire to ensure that *all* Americans receive the effective, compassionate medical treatment they deserve.

You will read in this memoir the story of a young boy whose early years were filled with obstacles to success. You will read about a young man's struggle to overcome intolerance and ignorance to excel as a physician of the highest caliber. And you will read of a seasoned professional's unwavering dedication to his calling.

I first became acquainted with LaSalle Leffall when we were both American Cancer Society volunteers in the 1970s. His presidency of the organization in 1978 radically changed the cancer control landscape and shaped the way generations of researchers and medical practitioners would tackle issues of public health disparities in general. He knew there were disturbing gaps in cancer incidence and mortality between African-Americans and

whites. In fact, in the mid-1970s, he and his colleagues published one of the seminal papers on the subject, calling public
scrutiny to the disproportionate number of African-Americans
dying of breast, lung, prostate, and colorectal cancers. Further-
more, several of the potential reasons for health disparities that
he led the way in identifying have been borne out by subsequent
studies.

This focus on disparities proved to be much more than simply an innovative approach to cancer control. Indeed, it represented a complete paradigm shift in how we in the public health
arena approached prevention, early detection, and treatment for
not only cancer, but all diseases. The push to address the individual needs of specific groups of people—rather than entire
populations—was not easily embraced. At that time, the cancer
control community focused its energies on topics such as overall
prevention, screening, and treatment. LaSalle faced an uphill
battle to convince many established leaders in the cancer community to target a single group of people. Fortunately, he refused
to accept the status quo, and more progressive minds prevailed.

LaSalle realized the fruits of his labors when, in 1979, the
American Cancer Society hosted the world's first conference devoted exclusively to the cancer problem among African-
Americans. The National Conference on Meeting the Challenge
of Cancer Among Black Americans examined some of the root
causes of disparities, such as poverty and the lack of insurance
coverage, that too often lead to cancer being diagnosed at later—
and less treatable—stages. Participants left this meeting with a
clear call to action: Use what they had learned to heighten cancer awareness among African-American communities, educate
people about the need for prevention through healthy lifestyle
choices and early detection through screening, and lobby our nation's lawmakers to ensure that cancer research and control remain top priorities on the legislative agenda.

This conference not only informed our thinking about how
to treat and prevent cancer among African-Americans, but it also

guided our thoughts on how to care for other underserved ethnic, racial, and socioeconomic groups. Scores of programs and
services aimed at special populations have since evolved. And
while we still have a long way to go before disparities in the cancer burden are eliminated, we are narrowing the gap every day
through comprehensive research, education, advocacy, and service programs. LaSalle Leffall was the thought leader behind that
success.

But disparities in the cancer burden are not the only area in
which LaSalle has distinguished himself as a thought leader. His
has been among the most eloquent, persuasive voices calling for
our nation to act on what we know about cancer, and to translate
laboratory science and clinical knowledge into public policies
that save lives. He became one of the most influential public
health figures to identify cancer as a political, as well as a medical, issue. He fully understands the critical importance and
value of using advocacy as a force multiplier to achieve real
change in communities nationwide.

I again had the opportunity to work closely with LaSalle in
1998, when he helped found and later chaired the National Dialogue on Cancer, now known as C-Change. This landmark al-
liance of government, private, and nonprofit organizations is an
outstanding example of the power of collaboration to effect
change. It provides a forum in which national cancer leaders can
identify and act on the most promising opportunities to advance
progress against the disease. LaSalle, in concert with former
President George H. W. Bush and former First Lady Barbara
Bush, helped to create this collaborative concept and very
quickly worked to secure its earliest successes, including increased funding for cancer research and greater coverage of life-
saving cancer screenings.

These are just two areas in which I am intimately familiar
with Dr. LaSalle Leffall's visionary leadership. There are so
many more than space permits me to relate here. For example,
there is his leadership as an early advocate in the ongoing battle

to eliminate the global scourge of tobacco, his deep and long-standing commitment to eradicate breast cancer and support the women whose lives it touches, and his very public efforts to work with the media to educate people about the lifesaving value of being screened for colon cancer. For these reasons, and so many more, LaSalle Leffall has made an indelible mark on public health by refusing to accept the artificial "limits" placed on what is possible in saving lives and ending suffering. Though it is difficult to believe that any one mortal man can do so much good in just one career, he has—and our lives today are the better for it. It has been a sincere honor to know him and to count him as one of my dearest friends and colleagues.

FOREWORD

Claude H. Organ Jr., M.D., F.A.C.S.
Emeritus Professor
Department of Surgery
University of California-San Francisco, East Bay

> *"Greatness of the heart brings to a personal influence on patients and people a name that will live among them for one or more generations. When greatness of the head and heart continue together they bring immortality."*
> —William H. Ogilvie (1887–1971)

This autobiography, revealing as it does the personal and professional experiences of a great surgeon during the latter part of the twentieth century, represents the best of Americana. Indeed, Dr. LaSalle D. Leffall Jr.'s life has been a remarkable journey. His story is an historical part of the transformation of our society.

Born of modest circumstances, Leffall had, as the key to his later success, the educational direction of his parents. He benefited greatly by coming from an intact family, a stability he continues to this day in his respective roles as husband and father to wife Ruthie and son Donney. From his youthful days in rural Florida, his firm spiritual and academic background, combined with hard work, led him to pursue a career of professional excellence.

No Boundaries outlines in detail Leffall's educational experiences at Florida A&M College (along with his yokefellow George Rawls) and the Howard University College of Medicine, and his fellowship at Memorial Sloan-Kettering Cancer Center, among other life events. Leffall's pride in being a surgeon radiates throughout this book as he reflects on how he benefited from the advice of outstanding surgeons, particularly the legendary

Charles Drew. His training paid huge dividends, and loyalty called him back to his med school alma mater.

As one of the early surgeons to accept the designation of surgical oncology as a specialty, Leffall had two overarching goals: (1) an abiding concern for the dignity and quality of life of cancer patients, and (2) the elimination of disparities in cancer care for underrepresented minorities. *No Boundaries* relates his many outstanding professional efforts, which culminated in his election to the presidencies of the American College of Surgeons, the American Cancer Society, and the Society of Surgical Oncology. Leffall remained well-focused during these separate careers, and his autobiography modestly records an incredible number of "firsts" achieved during his lifetime.

LaSalle Leffall is a classic role model for young residents and medical students—black and white, male and female. His boundless energy has touched many lives, including my own. While his journey through life has given him numerous awards and honors and the opportunity to walk among kings, princesses, and presidents, he has not lost the common touch. To top it off, *No Boundaries* will make for good reading.

FOREWORD

Thomas R. Russell, M.D., F.A.C.S.
Executive Director
American College of Surgeons

In the following pages, Dr. LaSalle D. Leffall Jr. recounts his triumphant journey from cleaning the segregated waiting rooms of a physician's office as a youth in the rural South (mostly because he yearned to be in a medical setting) to becoming one of the nation's, and the world's, foremost surgical educators and leaders. This autobiography is appropriately titled. Young Leffall acquired from his parents the belief that he could transcend the prejudices and stereotypes that pervaded this country's culture. Both were educators who believed that the racial walls of disparity could crumble under the weight of solid education and hard work. Their bedrock values, combined with his own agile mind and optimistic nature, clinched his success at overcoming boundaries.

As an adult, Dr. Leffall often found the medical profession's limited ability to understand, prevent, and cure disease as frustrating and troublesome as racial intolerance. As a cancer surgeon and surgical educator, he has brushed aside the social and political barriers that far too often prohibited many people in this country from succeeding in the surgical profession. His excellent surgical, diplomatic, and teaching skills, as well as his "can-do" attitude, have allowed him to break through the color barrier within many medical organizations. In the process, Dr. Leffall has opened doors of opportunity for generations of African-American surgeons.

Throughout his career, Dr. Leffall has won the respect and admiration of his patients, residents, and peers. Few surgeons are as highly esteemed and well loved. Indeed, he has served as a source of inspiration to nearly every surgeon who has had the pleasure of training under him or hearing one of his brilliant lectures. There is little doubt in my mind that the patients to whom he has provided care have equal respect and admiration for him. This autobiography is just one of the many "grace notes" that Dr. Leffall has contributed to all our lives. He has touched everyone who has had the distinction and privilege of knowing him, working with him, learning from him, and receiving care from him in intangible and indescribable ways.

ACKNOWLEDGMENTS

My sister, Dolores C. Leffall, Ph.D., was immensely helpful in the difficult task of researching the history of our family for this book, and I am deeply grateful to her. Her thoroughness and tenacity allowed me to assemble what had previously been a largely unwritten record. I would also like to thank my son, LaSalle D. ("Donney") Leffall III for his invaluable insights into the many versions of this manuscript.

I am grateful also to my maternal aunts, Edith Jordan and Eleanor Lee, and to my cousin Geneva Williams for information about the Jordan family; to my Aunt Beaulah Sanders, my father's only sister, and to my cousins Calloway Leffall Sr. and Berdie Leffall Pierce for collecting additional information about the Leffall family; to Sam Betsey, Blucher Lines, and Julia Woodward, for historical background about my hometown of Quincy, Florida; to William Dandy, my fraternity brother, for information about college activities; to Charlotte Bickett and Mary Brooks-Tapscott for research about Howard University's medical school and various cancer organizations; and to Diane Hawkins and Cathryn DeShields for their assistance in typing my manuscript.

Special thanks goes to my administrative secretary Michele K. Berry for her cool head and amazing organizational skills in tracking this work through many drafts, always with a smile.

I want to thank the following people for encouraging me to write this book: William Flynn and Thomas Moran; Caroline and Kate Sedgwick, who lent support to this project when it was just an inchoate idea; the late Katharine Graham, author of her own *Personal History*, who provided a model memoir and who told me to persevere because the result would be worth the effort; John O'Connor, who provided additional guidance through his memoirs; Jane Nevins of the Dana Foundation, who offered helpful advice on context; Earl G. Graves of *Black Enterprise* magazine, who supported this effort from its earliest stages; and Howard University President H. Patrick Swygert, who provided sterling support when my own commitment to this autobiographical endeavor was wavering. I owe all of them a debt of gratitude.

Thanks are due to friends Joan and Bernie Carl, Claire and Warren Cox, Shannon and Richard Fairbanks, Lucia and Joseph Henderson, Carol and Peter Kaplan, Hillie Mahoney, Joan and David Maxwell, Margaret and Armando Ortiz, and Tricia and Frank Saul—who generously provided escapes where I could reflect and work on these memoirs. To my dear friend Pat Hass, who suggested that I write and publish this memoir and who has been diligently involved from the beginning, offering unstinting professional advice—all I can say is that without her direction and expert advice this book would never have been completed.

Kenneth Mason provided wise counsel when the manuscript was in its embryonic stage, and my agent Kristen Auclair gave me the benefit of her superb editorial eye. Thank you both. And I am deeply grateful to professors Fred Irby III and Charlie Young of Howard University's Department of Music and its jazz ensemble for presenting a concert of an original composition entitled *Verzierungen* ("Grace Notes") by Dr. Frederick Tillis, professor emeritus, as a personal tribute to me prior to publication of this book. Thanks also to Dr. Eddie Henderson, noted jazz trumpeter and one of my former students (class of 1968), who also participated in the program.

My profound gratitude goes to Howard University Press director D. Kamili Anderson and to her editorial assistants Keasha Dumas, Jamie Walker, and Lenda Hill, who each exhibited delightful mixtures of enthusiasm and diligence in the face of resource challenges that would have made other publishing professionals cringe. Their commitment to excellence reflects the high standards set by Howard University and its scholarly offspring. The editors assigned to this project, Rachael Byrd and William Patrick, guided my words to higher ground with grace and compassion. Michael Putzel's professional competence and masterly editorial skills further allowed my thoughts to be cogently expressed in the written word. All of their efforts on my behalf have enlightened and uplifted me.

LDL
Washington, D.C.

PREFACE

I have often been asked to write an autobiography. I had previously refused because I thought it would appear self-serving, but my friend, Knopf editor Pat Hass, emphasized that my writing this memoir would be merely another way of teaching and conveying the themes that I have long stressed to my students—namely, excellence in all endeavors, advocacy for high quality health care, and mentoring for young professionals.

When I was born in the Deep South at the beginning of the Great Depression, the opportunities for a black person to rise to the zenith of a profession—any profession—were too small to measure. Yet if anyone ever told me that, I don't remember it. My parents certainly didn't. They believed in the American work ethic, in justice, and in the providence of an abiding Christian faith. I never doubted them. While I was growing up in the 1930s, '40s and '50s, so was America. The Jim Crow laws that governed where we blacks lived, went to school, sat in the movie theater, and yes, even where we were buried, gave way to a new system of open access.

Knocking down legal barriers, of course, didn't end discrimination or segregation overnight. African-Americans, as a group, are still struggling with that. But my career demonstrates that we can overcome the impediments to progress through determination, discipline, and the good will of colleagues and friends. I can't say that I was never discouraged, but I have never wavered in my conviction that, as my father said, "With a good education and hard work, combined with honesty and integrity, there are no boundaries."

I have enjoyed what can only be described as a fulfilling career—multiple careers, really—as a cancer surgeon, a professor of surgery, and leader of not one but several national organizations dedicated to conquering cancer and advancing my profession. From my earliest days tutoring returned veterans in college and leading fellow students on the "cadaver walk" to hone their knowledge of anatomy, I've treasured my role as teacher and mentor. Someone once calculated that in my forty-four years on the surgical faculty, I have taught over 4,200 of the 7,500 medical students who have graduated from Howard University's medical school since its founding in 1868. I have further assisted in training 260 of the 296 surgical residents (46 of whom were women) who completed their training in our department. I pride myself on having a respectful and affectionate relationship with my students, but they have always known from the start that I have high expectations of them—expectations that they are required to meet.

"There comes a time," wrote the American novelist James Salter, "when you realize that everything is a dream, and only those things preserved in writing have any possibility of being real." I have lived a dream for more than seven decades. In that time, I have saved many lives and comforted many patients whom I could not save. I have taught thousands of medical students to do what I myself have done over the years. I can only hope that I have helped people throughout the world understand, as I firmly believe, that we each have within us the power to defeat the most terrifying disease of our time. The dawn of a new world, free of cancer, is within our reach. Taking the time to write the story of my life has helped make that dream even more real for me. I hope my doing so will persuade others that they, too, can surmount any barriers that confront them.

1

Code Yellow! —
Equanimity Under Duress

It was a warm Saturday night, not unusual for Washington, D.C., in the springtime, but the hospital operating room wasn't air-conditioned, and everyone in it was hot and sweaty under the broiling surgery lights. My shift had started at 6:00 that morning, and by 8:00 in the evening I was exhausted. I had spent seven hours on one procedure alone, all of them on my feet, helping to remove a large tumor of the esophagus from an emaciated older man. The tumor had extended into his surrounding heart and lung tissues, which had made removing it extremely complicated and tedious.

I was a junior surgical resident at the time, in my third year of specialty training, and as was customary, our surgical residency team was closely supervised by more senior and experienced surgeons. Together we managed the extensive dissection and resection to remove the cancer, then reattach the remaining esophagus to the stomach.

As we closed and sutured the patient's chest and abdomen, all I wanted to do was grab something to eat and head straight to bed in the dormitory-like quarters reserved for residents and interns.

Yet, as my mind drifted off to the delicious idea of food and sleep, I heard my name over the hospital speaker system. I was being paged. I was needed in the emergency room, stat—immediately.

When I arrived in the ER I saw several police officers guarding four patients on gurneys. There were three men and one woman, all soaked in blood from gunshot wounds. They were agitated and combative. A fifth was already in the operating room, where the chief resident was trying to save his life. The police told us all five of the young people had been drinking heavily at a private party when shooting broke out. Illegal drugs figured in the fracas as well. None of the patients would give us any information, and one in particular, a young man of seventeen or eighteen, was so worked up that he had to be restrained, despite his serious wounds.

The chief resident told me to scrub for surgery right away and start on the young man strapped to the gurney. The hospital's other chief resident, who was on call, and an attending surgeon were on their way in, but we didn't have time to wait for them.

I swallowed hard. Instead of food and rest, I was about to receive my baptism in blood. I had never worked on a life-threatening case like this without more experienced surgeons at my side. In the normal course of training it would be another year before I would be entrusted with anything so serious on my own. But there wasn't time to think about that or about how tired I was.

Assisting me in the operating room were a first-year resident and a medical student. We scrubbed while the nurses prepared the patient. He had been shot in the abdomen and showed all the signs of serious blood loss. His blood pressure was falling, he had a rapid pulse, and both his hemoglobin and hematocrit values were low. He might die at any moment.

I steadied myself as I made a long, midline incision, opening his abdomen from the lower part of the breastbone, curving around the navel, then extending down to the pubic bone. I was a self-confident young doctor, at least where matters of science and medicine were concerned, and I trusted my training. My adrenalin was pumping, offsetting the mental and physical fatigue.

As my scalpel moved smoothly down the man's body, the incision deepened and blood spurted out of the cavity and gushed over the sides of the wound. I quickly inserted the absorbent cloth pads known as packs in the abdominal cavity to soak up the bright red liquid and carefully removed them to expose the internal tissue. I discovered the patient was bleeding from his liver and from the mesentery, folds of tissue that are filled with arteries and veins to nourish the small and large intestines. Blood quickly filled the cavity again, blocking my view of the organs inside. I felt lightheaded as it rose toward my hands and spilled over onto the operating table and splattered on the floor. He was losing blood by the pint. I suddenly wasn't sure what to do. My confidence evaporated as I realized I could easily lose my cool and this man would die in my care.

The first-year resident and the medical student held retractors, pulling back the incision to expose the space for me as I suctioned off the blood and identified the source. I clamped the severed vessels, while packing the liver with pads to prevent further bleeding. I moved on to tie off the bleeding vessels in the mesentery when the on-call chief resident and attending surgeon opened the door to the operating room to let me know they had arrived and were getting ready as quickly as they could. They scrubbed in less than the usual ten minutes, donned surgical gowns and gloves, and hurried into the operating field around the patient. Help had arrived.

My momentary uncertainty was forgotten. The rhythms and procedures of my training, so vital to quick, decisive action in an emergency, had kicked in, and I moved one step at a time to stop the bleeding and save a young life. I confess, however, that I heaved a silent breath of relief as my more experienced colleagues joined me at the operating table. With calm, deliberate maneuvers and unflappable demeanor, they assumed control of the room and everyone in it. Our patient survived the surgery and, despite a rather stormy course during the next three weeks, he walked out of the hospital feeling fine.

The surgeons' confidence and calm as they took over to complete the operation still illuminate my thinking as I look back on more than fifty-seven years in medicine. I call it "equanimity under duress," one of the most desirable qualities in a surgeon— or in anyone, for that matter.

Ernest Hemingway, a great admirer of courage whether in war or in the bullring, called it "grace under pressure." Professionalism in any field requires being able to react to crises in a temperate manner. One must think clearly and act appropriately under the worst conditions. In our personal lives as well, getting agitated or losing one's control almost always causes us to do or say something we later regret. In the operating room it is not simply a manifestation of personal courage, it is the ability to execute procedures and exercise judgment when the stakes are highest. To panic, or even get flustered, when a patient goes into cardiac arrest or bursts a blood vessel may prove fatal for the patient.

When physicians—at least those of my generation—hear the term "equanimity," they immediately think of Sir William Osler, the first professor of medicine at Johns Hopkins University and later Regius professor of medicine at Oxford. I first heard of him as I sat listening to Dean Joseph L. Johnson welcome our entering class at Howard University's College of Medicine in 1948. I later learned Osler's credo: "In the physician or surgeon no quality takes rank with imperturbability . . . which means coolness and presence of mind under all circumstances. . . . The physician who has the misfortune to be without it . . . loses rapidly the confidence of his patients."

Osler called it *Aequanimitas,* or equanimity. In his valedictory address at the University of Pennsylvania in 1889, just before he joined the faculty at Hopkins, he described the concept and attributed it to the dying summation of the gentle Roman ruler Antoninus Pius, who died in 161 A.D.

Between 1932 and 1953, approximately 150,000 graduating medical school seniors across the nation received, along with their diplomas, a copy of Osler's book as a gift from their schools. It was entitled *Aequanimitas: With Other Addresses to Medical Students, Nurses, and Practitioners of Medicine.* Howard didn't give out the book at graduation, but I received one later. One of my anatomy professors, Dr. Ruth Lloyd, knew of my interest and gave me a copy from her late husband's personal library.

"Aequanimitas" has been the guiding principle of my surgical career, working primarily with patients stricken by cancer or calamity. My ultimate task, as I see it, has been to restore to their lives the calm and serenity that I require myself to demonstrate at all times while they are under my care. My students and fellow surgeons joke that my style doesn't always seem to encourage calm. Indeed, they sometimes point out that my most memorable instruction, whether in the OR or on grand rounds with my students is: "Quickly! Quickly!" To my nurses, I try always to add, "Please," but I confess that if a tongue-tied student doesn't respond fast enough when I ask a question while making rounds, I may simply move on to someone else with the simple command, "Next." Underlying those demands for haste, however, is calm—and the knowledge that in the process, I am subtly teaching that same equanimity I so value in my own life.

I believe now, on reflection, that the calm I have practiced all these years was rooted not in my medical school training but actually grew from seeds planted much earlier, when I was growing up in the segregated South, where Jim Crow was always at hand, ready to ruin a child who got careless. There, I learned, the key to success was not anger or panic, but quiet determination.

2

My Beginnings

Most of what I know about my family comes from a rich oral tradition passed from one generation to the next because there aren't many records. Nonetheless, I am a product of a family with deep roots in the American South, and what I know of my forebears, their strength, resilience, and optimism in harder times than I have ever known certainly has helped shape me and has guided my career. My own desire to achieve and succeed surely grew from theirs. The story of my family is also a story about our nation's ability to change and grow.

My mother's grandfather, Paul Moore, was born a slave in Talladega County, Alabama, in 1825. He belonged to a white man named Gabriel Moore, and when Moore's daughter, Lucy Jane, was married, Moore gave my great-grandfather to her as a wedding gift. Lucy Jane's husband was Dr. Fleming Jordan (pronounced "Jerdan" in that part of the South), and following common practice Paul's surname changed to that of his new owner. My great-grandfather therefore became known as Paul Jordan. The custom of requiring slaves to bear their masters' names—if they were given surnames at all—and changing those names as slaves were conveyed from owner to owner, make tracing African-American genealogy a complicated affair.

Dr. Jordan and his family moved to Madison County, Alabama, and settled on a plantation near the town of Maysville. There Paul met and married my great-grandmother, Flora, one of the doctor's illegitimate daughters born to his slaves and, by law, slaves themselves. Paul and Flora had five daughters and six sons, one of whom was my grandfather, Jeremiah, born in 1861.

My other great-grandmother on my mother's side, Ezell Meade, was born in Bellefonte, Jackson County, Alabama, in 1858. She was the daughter of Maria Meade, a slave belonging to cotton plantation owner Lem Meade. After the Civil War, Ezell married a newly freed slave from the same plantation, a young man named Jeff. He and Ezell Meade had two sons and four daughters, one of whom was my grandmother, Callie.

Freed as a young boy at the end of the Civil War and eager for an education, Jeremiah Jordan attended high school at Huntsville Normal School. He was the only member of his family to go beyond the elementary grades, and he became the lone teacher in a one-room school in Paint Rock, Alabama. One of his students was Callie Meade, daughter of Jeff and Ezell. Smitten by her beauty, charm, and wholesomeness, Jeremiah married her in 1892, when she was only sixteen. He was almost twice her age. Their marriage was blessed with nine children, one of whom was my mother, Martha, who was born fifteen minutes later than her twin brother Harris, who never missed an opportunity to remind her that she was younger than he was. Jeremiah Jordan later taught at Flint River Baptist Church School, where my mother and her siblings received their early education.

My father's family was also rooted in Alabama. A French plantation owner named Leffall purchased a slave family—my forebears—from a slave owner named Bull, who lived near Tuskegee, Alabama. After the Civil War the newly freed Leffalls traveled several hundred miles to the Furrah Cotton Plantation, a small farming community in Mount Pleasant, Texas, that gave former slaves an opportunity to farm and receive a share of the harvest.

My father, LaSalle, the fourth of ten surviving sons, was born December 5, 1899. My grandfather named my father LaSalle because he thought that the two names, LaSalle and Leffall, had a nice sound. Some family members also claim that we were named after René-Robert Cavelier, Sieur de La Salle, the French explorer who got lost looking for the Mississippi but landed in Texas and established France's claim to much of the North American interior.

My father, like his parents, was born just outside Marshall, Texas, in a farming community known as Mount Pleasant or, to some, Elysian Fields, where his father had purchased a 350-acre farm after years as a sharecropper. He attended a one-room public school that went only to the eighth grade.

Growing up, I was told that my father ran away from home because an uncle told him if he stayed in Mount Pleasant he could not aspire to become anything except a farmer. Since my father had spoken so often about getting a college education, he should just leave home and not tell anyone. Only in conducting research for these memoirs did I learn that his family knew about his departure. The earlier story about his running away is what really influenced me because it showed an emphasis on education and risk taking. These attributes remain with me even today.

He left home after the eighth grade, at the age of fifteen, to enroll in the demonstration high school and later the college at Prairie View, some 130 miles away. He earned his tuition and board by working in the school's dining room and laundry and received his B.S. degree in Vocational Agriculture in 1925.

My father had no middle name until the early 1920s, when he saw the name Doheny in a newspaper while he was a student at Prairie View State College in Texas. He thought the name LaSalle Doheny Leffall had a certain ring to it and claimed it as his own. The subject of the article, Edward L. Doheny, was the brilliant, driven entrepreneur who created Los Angeles' first oil boom and became one of the wealthiest and most controversial businessmen in the nation. Although eventually acquitted of bribery charges, Doheny was forever linked to the infamous Teapot Dome scandal involving the award of oil leases on federal land during the Harding administration. I was named for my father, and I named my son LaSalle Doheny Leffall III.

He went on to Iowa State in Ames, Iowa, the nation's oldest land-grant college, recognized as one of the best agricultural schools in the world. Iowa State's best-known graduate then, as now, was George Washington Carver, its first black student and a pioneer in peanut farming. My father put himself through graduate school working as a waiter and handyman in local restaurants and hotels. He landed a job teaching vocational agriculture at Alabama Normal Institute near Huntsville in 1926.

There he met Martha Jordan, a pretty country girl who was visiting her sister Edith, a student at the school. He began courting Martha at her home in Maysville and found her strikingly intelligent beyond her years. Mother was an extrovert who loved meeting people and made friends easily. She also baked delicious cakes, and my father had a serious sweet tooth. With his erudite deportment, steady demeanor, and new two-door Chevrolet roadster, he captured her attention in turn. He took her to plays, recitals, and sporting events at Normal and in the surrounding townships. They often drove around Maysville, and on several occasions visited my mother's oldest sister Beatrice and her family. Not to be overlooked as a supporting factor in their courtship, my mother's mother, Callie, also was fond of my father.

LaSalle Doheny Leffall and Martha Jordan were married on May 18, 1928. The bride was just nineteen years old. The following fall they moved back to Ames in order for my father to continue his graduate studies. Accompanying them to Iowa and later to Florida, where my father taught at Florida A&M College in Tallahassee, was my mother's youngest sister, Eleanor, who also planned to continue her education wherever the family settled.

My mother's father, Jeremiah, himself a teacher, told his children constantly and at length that blacks should take advantage of increased opportunities in education, management, law—and yes, even medicine. Mother had been one of his best pupils, and after she finished sixth grade, he enlisted her to help him with the students in earlier grades. She was later asked to teach in one of the nearby rural grade schools and continued teaching most of her life. For years she worked with just a high school diploma that she obtained by examination and an associate degree she received studying at home and taking "short courses," or correspondence classes she could work on during the summer or after helping the rest of us with our homework in the evenings. My father, who married her before she could enter college, always urged her to get a bachelor's degree, and in 1946 when my sister and I were teenagers she finally earned a degree in elementary education from FAMC. I remember her as an outgoing, effervescent person who always had a hug for her friends and a ready smile.

Mother had a sense of style that she must have picked up from her keen observation of others because she had grown up on a farm. She taught, either at the elementary or high school level, from the early 1930s until the mid-1980s, when she was in her seventies. She even found time to do graduate work while teaching. There were, of course, far too many students to mention over the course of more than a half century of teaching, but she loved telling one story about a boy from the "quarters," a low-income area of Quincy, who was raised by a single mother and, with lots of encouragement from my mother and other teachers, went on to FAMU and Meharry Medical College. Dr. Willie Adams became one of the most successful OB-GYN specialists in Albany, Georgia. Years later he returned to Quincy in a limousine to take his three favorite teachers, including my mother, out to lunch to express his gratitude. In February 2004

Adams was elected mayor of Albany. Mother would have been so proud.

My father had a one-year stint teaching vocational agriculture at Florida A&M College (known in those days as "Famcee" for its initials, FAMC) and in 1953 gained university status, becoming FAMU. I was born there, in the hospital on campus, on May 22, 1930. Tallahassee was one of a handful of communities in the region that had a hospital for blacks in those days, and I was among a relative few to be born in a hospital. Dr. L. H. B. Foote, the hospital's medical director, delivered me and loved to tell people for years afterward that I made so much noise at birth he knew I'd be a good public speaker or singer. Dr. Foote, who had graduated five years before from Howard University College of Medicine, was already a family friend and became a role model, staunch supporter, and valuable adviser as I was growing up. As the chief medical officer in that small college hospital, he did more to improve the health care for black citizens in Tallahassee than any other individual during the early part of the century.

We were only in Tallahassee for a year, because while teaching there, my father was offered the position of principal of the black high school in Eustis, a small town in central Florida. He liked teaching but thought that being in charge of a high school was an opportunity to affect the lives of more black boys and girls than serving on the faculty at the college level. The principal position in Eustis was one of the few opportunities open to a well-educated young black man in the South. There wasn't much housing available in Eustis, but one of the benefits he was offered to entice him to take the job was the chance to live in the school. For two years our family was housed in vacant classrooms converted to living space, and we cooked in the school kitchen. We were actually luckier than many of the local residents because the school had indoor plumbing.

My sister Dolores was born in Orlando in October 1931, and the next we moved to Quincy, a small city in Gadsden

County, where my father was principal of a larger high school. Dolores and I grew up in Quincy, twenty miles from the state capital of Tallahassee in the northwest part of the state known as the Florida Panhandle. The region has more in common with its neighboring states of Georgia and Alabama than with the urban areas and popular tourist attractions to the south that most Northerners bring to mind when they think of Florida.

It was the beginning of the Great Depression, and segregation ruled our lives then, but my memories of Quincy are generally fond ones. I loved growing up there. Many of my classmates have remained close friends for years, although our numbers have dwindled with time.

We lived in a modest house with a separate garage just off the main highway through town and a backyard where I played horseshoes and shot marbles with my friends. We always had a car. I remember a new Ford in 1936 and a new Plymouth in 1941. Both years we traveled to Marshall, Texas. Those were the only trips I remember to my father's boyhood home.

Gadsden County had a population of about 30,000 in the 1930s. Quincy, with approximately 12,000 people, was 60 percent black. Some of the white families in the county became wealthy raising tobacco, the area's primary industry, but quite a few also benefited from their association with Mark Welch ("Pat") Munroe, president of the Quincy State Bank from 1892 to 1940. Munroe liked the management of a young soda pop manufacturer in Atlanta called the Coca-Cola Company, and he thought people would always be willing to pay a nickel for a cool drink on a hot day. He invested in the company when it went public in 1919 and urged many of his friends, relatives, and customers at the bank to do the same. Counting Quincy's Coca-Cola millionaires is still a local parlor game, although in Quincy, as elsewhere in the South, the word is usually pronounced "Co-cola." It was rumored that at least one black family got rich by buying Co-cola stock, but we were never able to confirm that.

In my youth, the two-story, dull-yellow brick county court-house, its distinctive cupola with clocks facing in all four directions, stood in the center of town, surrounded by Quincy's stores and businesses. One block away was South Adams Street, where most of the "colored" businesses were located: a drycleaner, several barbershops and restaurants, and a drugstore owned by Dr. W. S. Stevens, the city's lone "colored" physician. Dr. Stevens and his wife were close friends of our family. My mother was especially fond of Mrs. Stevens, who became my godmother.

Doc Stevens was probably the most prominent black man in the county, and he played a major role in local civic and community activities. The blacks-only high school was named in his honor. His drugstore not only was the place where blacks came to purchase medicine, it was the hot spot for Quincy's black youth to gather. We enjoyed sandwiches, soft drinks, and ice cream and listening to popular tunes on the jukebox. I remember it, too, because Doc Stevens often told me how much he loved practicing medicine—and that I could get great joy from a career in medicine.

I was three weeks old when my mother took me north to Alabama on the train to visit my grandmother, aunts, uncles, and cousins on a cotton farm in Maysville, outside the city of Huntsville. I don't remember that trip, of course, but I have fond memories of Maysville. Dolores and I spent the next eleven summers there. In the fertile bottomland we discovered the smokehouse, the harrow, the rolling store, cows lowing at sundown—and how remarkably refreshing cool well water can be on a hot summer day. We looked forward to Saturdays, when my grandmother, aunt and uncles drove us into Huntsville to a place called the "Sweet Shop," where they indulged us in ice cream sundaes, malted milk shakes, floats, and cherry Cokes, made at the fountain. On Sundays we went to church, in either Flint, Hurricane, or Brownsboro. My mother's oldest sister, Aunt Bea, lived on a neighboring 115-acre farm with her husband,

Uncle Isham, and their eight children. We loved to visit them to ride the huge tractor, romp in the fresh-smelling hay, and go on endless outdoor adventures with our cousins. Without much formal education, but with plenty of intelligence, pride, self-respect, and dignity, the Jordans showed us how a black family in the Deep South could live a rewarding, happy life through hard work, keeping out of debt and being kind to each other and to outsiders. I vividly remember they got up early in the morning, worked until the noon meal, went back into the fields, and didn't come home till supper. They took their religion seriously and led their lives full of spirituality.

In 1941 my mother's family moved to Chicago, where two of my aunts already had settled. For the next five years my sister and I spent our summers in the Windy City, a big, bustling metropolis that opened a new world for us after life in Quincy and our visits to Maysville. We marveled at the sights and sounds of the annual Bud Billiken Parade, one of Chicago's largest, organized by the black community in celebration of the mythical "patron saint of the little guy," first featured in the renowned black newspaper, *The Chicago Defender.* Over and over again, we visited the city's massive libraries, its spacious parks, the Brookfield Zoo and Riverview Amusement Park, and we never grew tired of what we saw, felt, and heard. Knowing few children of my age, I spent several hours weekdays in the local library reading works by black writers including Richard Wright, Zora Neale Hurston, Jean Toomer, Phillis Wheatley, and Langston Hughes.

Back home, my parents, both educators, emphasized to my sister and me the importance of education from our earliest days. It was their strategy for success, both for themselves and their children, and they were unrelenting. We learned to read early and were expected to excel in our studies. As a result, I began first grade at age five, skipped second grade and finished high school in three years. By the time I was fifteen, I was ready to head off to college.

When we were in the fourth and sixth grades, Dolores and I were required to learn a new word every weekday, not including the vocabulary we were learning in school. At dinner each evening, we were expected to use our new words in sentences to show that we understood their meanings. This exercise stimulated a thirst for knowledge that persists today. Sixty years later I can still spell—and define—words such as apostasy, cynosure, eristic, morganatic, recondite, querulous, threnody, and uxorious.

Our parents wanted us to be inquisitive and to ask questions. When we wanted to know something, we were always referred to our two-volume *Lincoln Library of Essential Information*, our equivalent, in those days, of the Internet children use today. I still remember one parent or the other saying, "Look it up in the Lincoln Library." Those two volumes, a bit tattered now with the gloss worn off their once-shiny black covers, stand today on a prominent shelf in my personal library.

Unlike some families in those days, in which the male child was pressed harder academically, in ours Dolores and I were treated equally. Our parents wanted us both to pursue higher learning. While I was an undergraduate and in postgraduate medical training, my sister earned her B.A. in Sociology from FAMC, then a master's degree from Indiana University, and her Ph.D. from Rutgers in Library Science.

Our parents always tried to have dinner with us. Over our usual meals of beef, pork, chicken, or fish; collard, mustard or turnip greens; potatoes or rice and milk—always milk—they would ask us about the pressing issues of the day and about what we had learned in school. We went over our new words, too, of course, but dinner wasn't just drill time. My father and mother spoke often to us about moral, ethical, and spiritual values. It may seem old-fashioned today, but the virtues of integrity, honesty, loyalty, generosity, responsibility, and civility were frequent topics at our dinner table. As for the food, I remember T-bone steak as my absolute favorite, and we had it at least once a week.

Daddy, as I always called my father, had a knack for stimulating conversation, and he led the discussions. He and I didn't always see eye-to-eye when he was empathic, but in his calm and steady manner, he delivered advice in cool, soothing tones I can still hear today:

"Always be willing to compromise to reach your goals, but never compromise on principle."

"Maintain civility and, above all, don't be petty in your actions."

"Never fail to express thanks in the written or spoken word when someone does something nice for you."

"When you're wrong, admit it. Apologize, cut your losses, and move on."

I know now he was right, and my father remains my greatest hero. He spoke often about loyalty—not the type based on one's position but rather that based on one's principles. He often told me that if he had to choose between an associate who was mediocre but loyal and one who was superior but disloyal, he would choose the less talented loyal colleague without question.

"It's the loyal person you can count on and who will not betray you," he'd say. I always suspected that at some point a colleague had betrayed him, but he never let on if that was the case. Friendship, like fidelity, was another fundamental tenet. I once came across something he had written in a classmate's autograph book upon graduation from college in 1925. "A friend," he had penned in his distinctive handwriting, "is dearer than the light of day, and it were better for us that there were no sun than that we should be without friends." A bit florid, perhaps, but he meant it, and I came to understand the treasure friends are when you need them.

I knew my father had grown up poor and learned the value of work from his own father. During one of the two visits we made to his family's home in Marshall, my father told us that when he'd left home to go away to school his family gave him thirty dollars, all it could afford to help him on his way.

He took pride in telling us he'd worked his way through school and let us know in no uncertain terms we were to earn our own spending money. I had four different jobs during my school years: delivering packages for Crouch's drugstore, working as a line inspector checking soda pop for gross impurities at the NuGrape bottling plant, cleaning a doctor's office, and priming tobacco on a farm one summer. Tobacco leaves grow from a single tall stalk, and picking—or priming—the leaves is done from the bottom up. We started, early in the harvest season, by breaking off the "sand leaves," the two or three small leaves closest to the ground on each plant. To get to the sand leaves meant bending from the waist almost to the ground and moving from plant to plant through an entire field. At the end of the day, my back hurt so much I could hardly stand. I vowed that summer I would find a better way to spend my life.

The most frustrating of my early jobs was cleaning the physician's office, the work I hoped would be the most fun. I was thirteen and was already interested in studying medicine. Dr. Fain Godard, a white physician, knew I was keen on medicine and offered me the job sweeping up and dusting his office and waiting rooms. I was fascinated by the books in his library, the smell of antiseptics and all the medical instruments in the examining room. It was the waiting rooms that I found objectionable. There were two of them, as was customary then in the South, one "white" and one "colored." The white waiting room was spacious, with nice furniture and current magazines. The colored waiting room was cramped and dingy, with tired old furniture and worn, outdated periodicals. I found the disparities demeaning and realized that unequal treatment could make black children feel worthless and inferior. I was fortunate, of course, to have strong parents and teachers to bolster my self-esteem, but not all my peers had such sturdy support.

I loved the medical atmosphere and delighted in watching the looks on patients' faces as they left the office, usually relieved and pleased with their visit to the doctor. I just wanted no part of those two unequal waiting rooms, however. After a few months, I thanked Dr. Godard for the opportunity to work in his office and gave up the job without summoning the courage to tell him why I was leaving.

My schoolmates and I lived under the so-called "separate-but-equal" school system prevalent at the time. Given our tender ages, we were oblivious to the most brutal aspects of racism and discrimination. In this sense, then, I guess I had what could be considered a "normal" childhood for middle-class black youth of the day. We participated in classroom activities, staged school plays, and engaged in schoolroom hijinks. We were well aware of the decidedly unequal nature of public accommodations and facilities around us, and we knew there were places where we were forbidden to go. As I reflect on those times, however, I recall that knowing the rules only made me more determined to succeed.

Our teachers, more than I realized at the time, struggled against significant obstacles to nurture our ambitions and help me and my classmates look positively at life. With constant scrutiny at home and at school, we just had to be the best. I accepted that credo, like segregation, as a fact of life. We learned about the many black men and women who had paved the way for us by exceeding all expectations. Figures such as Frederick Douglass, Paul Robeson, Mary McLeod Bethune, George Washington Carver, W. E. B. DuBois, Marian Anderson, Joe Louis, William Hastie, Thurgood Marshall, and Ernest Everett Just were my heroes and heroines growing up. I studied their lives then, and their accomplishments inspire me still.

I especially admired the intellect of Howard University biologist Ernest Everett Just. He loved the written word and the dramatic arts, excelled in Greek and history at Dartmouth, yet he made his most important contribution in science. My aunt bought me a copy of Just's *The Biology of the Cell Surface*, one of the seminal treatises of molecular biology at that time. I devoured the book from cover to cover as if it were a novel. I

fantasized about the day when I, like Just, would make a brilliant discovery or conduct research that would shape the future.
I was proud that Just was a black man and, more than that, a
black man whose achievements far outweighed race.

For some reason, the persistence that has guided me in almost every other aspect of my life didn't carry over to athletics. I
just could never get serious about participating in sports activities. However, I always enjoyed watching various sporting
events. Reading, on the other hand, was something I loved to do
from early childhood. Since black children were barred from the
city's public library, I had to rely on our ill-equipped school library and on the books my parents bought for my sister and me.
To keep up on the political and social issues of interest to blacks,
my family subscribed to not one but three black weekly newspapers: *The Pittsburgh Courier*, *The Chicago Defender*, and *The
Afro-American* of Baltimore. These stalwart, independent news
sources were vitally important to keep us informed about the
burgeoning civil rights activities of the '40s and '50s and the ongoing contributions of African-Americans in many arenas. My
father was partial to the *Defender* because it was the only black
newspaper he could get his hands on as a graduate student in
Iowa, and its December 22, 1928, issue featured his photograph
and a short article about a presentation he gave in Chicago on
vocational education.

One part of our family life that was never optional was
church. As children, we went to Sunday school and church services and received hours upon hours of instruction about the
Christian faith and doctrine in order to become baptized members of the Methodist Church. We learned that the essence of the
religious experience was reflected in how we treated our fellow
human beings, and respect for others was our guiding tenet.
These principles remain as strong as ever in my life.

After church, we often went to visit our parents' friends for
dinner. When I was eleven, we drove one Sunday to the home of
Mr. and Mrs. Roy Allen, who lived in the neighboring town of

Marianna. Mr. Allen, who was principal at his local all-black high school and also taught agriculture, was one of my father's colleagues, and I remember we had an unusually delicious dinner. On the drive home that evening, our parents were telling us about the importance of having friends like the Allens, and the two of us in the back seat began to nod off. My father turned on the radio and switched from station to station to locate some calming music, but all he could get was an announcer reading a news bulletin. It was December 7, 1941, and the Japanese had bombed Pearl Harbor.

I stirred from my half-sleep to listen to the feverish reports on our car radio. I had never heard of Pearl Harbor and had no idea where it was. My father pulled over to the side of the road and stopped for several minutes to listen to the details, then resumed our trip home in stunned silence.

The next day we gathered in the living room around our big floor model radio, a handsome wooden console made by Atwater Kent, to hear President Franklin Roosevelt describe "December 7, 1941, a date that will live in infamy." It was a short speech that ended with the president asking Congress to declare a state of war between the United States and the Japanese empire. Although the enormity of the event was lost on my sister and me, we knew from our parents' anxious, worried faces that something horrible had happened.

Within months, the signs of mobilization appeared in town. I remember armored vehicles and military trucks rumbling through Quincy, presumably on their way to and from Dale Mabry Field, an Army Air Force training base in Tallahassee. Young men were ordered to register for the draft, and posters appeared trumpeting the war effort and urging citizens to "Buy Bonds" and "Save Rubber." We'd pick up old tires and turn them in to get paid and support the war effort.

I still remember the name of Captain Colin P. Kelly of nearby Madison County, Florida, one of the first heroes of the war. Kelly was a bomber pilot whose plane was hit by Japanese gunners as it returned to Clark Air Base in the Philippines after a bombing run on December 10, 1941, three days after Pearl Harbor. He stayed at the controls to keep the plane flying while his crew bailed out. The bomber exploded before he could parachute to safety.

I remember the early '40s for the good times as well. All the kids in my town looked forward to Quincy's annual tobacco festival, a chance to have some fun—at least relatively speaking, if not by today's measure. My friends and I would ride the Ferris wheel, the roller coaster, and the merry-go-round until we were dizzy. We'd scare each other at the haunted house and stuff ourselves with candy apples, popcorn, and cotton candy.

I loved the movies, and whenever I had some extra money would head to the Roxy, Quincy's "colored" movie theater. There, my friends and I would get caught up in the exciting worlds of the "sepia stars," such as Paul Robeson and Josephine Baker. We also went to the Shaw, a theater frequented by both blacks and whites. We had to sit in the balcony there, but we got to see movies starring Shirley Temple, Mickey Rooney, Roy Rogers, Buck Jones, and other favorites. A sad day for me was when my father reported that Buck Jones, one of the most popular cowboy actors of his day and a great favorite of mine, had burned to death at the Cocoanut Grove nightclub in Boston. The disaster occurred on November 28, 1942, less than a year into the war. It killed 492 people who were trapped by locked or blocked doors when a teenage bar boy struck a match that accidentally ignited the satin material lining the ceiling in the downstairs lounge. Years later, when I was taking the oral examination to become certified by the American Board of Surgery, I was asked several questions about the treatment of patients with major burns, and many of the answers stemmed from research by Harvard surgeons treating victims of that awful fire. When asked these questions I still recalled the Buck Jones story from my childhood.

My father was a stocky, six-foot-tall man, somewhat professorial in appearance and constantly in motion. He usually dressed in a suit or hickory-striped pants, as was fitting for a high school principal. On special occasions he wore his blue serge suit and black Florsheim shoes. He was well aware of the racial injustices of our time, but always encouraged us to prove our worth by performance and never use race as an excuse for under-achievement or failure. He encouraged us to fight for social justice by all legal means. He maintained we would never make any progress unless we had the law on our side and pointed to Thurgood Marshall, then counsel to the NAACP, and William H. Hastie, the first black federal judge in America, as black men who were using the legal system to advance civil rights. My father said that just doing your own part well enough would speed the change we all sought. Like an echo I can hear today, more than fifty years after his death, he would look us in the eye and tell us, always in the same words with the same inflection: "With a good education and hard work, combined with honesty and integrity, there are no boundaries."

The advice and support from our parents and teachers helped us confront social injustice. But we can never forget the thousands of men, women, and children of all races, some of whom made the ultimate sacrifice, who made the Civil Rights movement one of the shining victories of the twentieth century. We will be forever indebted to those valiant and brave souls who risked their lives in our quest for equality. And thus in Quincy today, there are no more segregated waiting rooms in doctors' offices or medical facilities. When a black child is first exposed to his or her doctor, there is no stigma of second-class citizenship. The last chief of surgery at the local hospital was a black woman, Dr. Jessie Furlow. The community has had black mayors, police chiefs, school superintendents, school board members, and city and county commissioners. Yet, who knows how many talented young boys or girls of my generation and before were dissuaded from pursuing careers in medicine or other professions because they couldn't see the opportunities beyond the obstacles?

I had a resolute family, visionary teachers, and the determination to succeed. I was most fortunate.

3

Destination: Med School

I was on my way home from school on a warm spring day when I stumbled on a robin that had broken its wing and was unable to fly. I picked it up and brought it home, hoping to make it better. I was nine years old, and that was the day I decided to become a doctor.

My father, who had worn a splint the year before for a sprained wrist, suggested that I splint the injured bird's broken appendage. Armed with wooden tongue depressors, string, and some stale crackers (in case my patient wanted something to eat after the surgery) I began to "operate." I splinted the bird's wing and fed it some of the crumbs from my pocket.

After a few days, the wing had healed enough for the bird to fly away. My first patient was on its way to recovery, and I was triumphant, telling my story to anyone who would listen—exaggerating each pre- and postoperative detail. I was hooked on healing, and I proudly announced to all my friends that I was going to become "*Dr. Leffall*"!

When the time came to take the first formal step toward my goal—an undergraduate premedical degree—Florida Agricultural and Mechanical College was an easy choice. It was then and remains Florida's only state-supported, historically black institution of higher education. My father had taught there, and he and Mother often attended the college's concerts, recitals, and homecoming football games. I had heard about "Famcee" all my life.

I was only fifteen, but I already knew that students who wanted to go on to medical school had to do well in "the three Ws." The three were not subjects but people: Ethan Earl Ware, biology; Lawrence Whitfield, anatomy and bacteriology; and Ralph Wardlow, chemistry. They were the science department's three most inspirational and demanding professors. Actually, by the time I arrived in September 1945, Ware was the only one still teaching there, but the reputation of the triumvirate was still intact. I walked onto campus as one of 432 new freshmen in a class swollen with veterans just home from overseas. The Germans had surrendered in May, the Japanese on September 12, and our college, like others throughout the country, was inundated by servicemen. In their twenties and thirties when the fighting ended, they had lost their youth in the war but were paid by the G.I. Bill to get an education and rebuild their interrupted lives. As the youngest in the class, I was the target of a lot of teasing that year because I was so young and inexperienced in the eyes of the vets. It didn't help that I was from a small town. My classmates treated me like a puppy wet behind the ears. The GIs particularly enjoyed talking about their romantic exploits, the great cities, and historical sites they had visited in Europe. "Youngblood," they told me, "you wouldn't know what we're talking about. But you'll learn when you get older." Their words stung at first. I had as much right to be at Famcee as they did, fifteen or not!

My attitude, of course, only fueled their teasing, but over time I learned to laugh along with them. There was a certain *esprit de corps* among that group of worldly, determined black men, many of whom—like me—had their hearts set on going to medical school. I was honored to be among them. They taught me not to take myself quite so seriously. In the long run that made my life easier—and a lot more fun. My personal victory came when some of the older guys asked me for help with their courses, especially the notoriously difficult zoology, chemistry, and French classes in which I did well.

My three years at FAMC—I was on the honors fast track—were among the best of my life. It was fascinating for a kid from a small town. There were bull sessions in the student union, dances, performances of the Playmakers Guild, fraternity parties, the debating society, athletic events, concerts, recitals, and work on the *Famcean* student newspaper. The possibilities seemed endless. Tallahassee was only twenty miles from Quincy and certainly no New York City, but in terms of sophistication it was light years ahead of my little hometown. I ate it up!

At Lee Hall I got to see and hear some of the finest classical singers and musicians in the country, beginning with the great soprano Dorothy Maynor, who performed on campus in the fall of my freshman year. There was Lillian Evanti, lyric coloratura soprano; Roland Hayes, tenor; Philippa Schuyler, a piano prodigy; and perhaps the greatest of all, Marian Anderson, contralto, who appeared at FAMC on November 18, 1947. That was years before the internationally acclaimed opera singer became the first black hired by New York's Metropolitan Opera, but she was already famous. On Easter Sunday, April 9, 1939, after the Daughters of the American Revolution barred her from performing at Constitution Hall, Ms. Anderson sang on the steps of the Lincoln Memorial before an integrated crowd of 75,000 people and a nationwide radio audience. The event, arranged by first lady Eleanor Roosevelt, was a landmark in the quest for social justice, and although I didn't hear the original concert, I certainly knew about it from the black newspapers we read at home, and seeing her perform was an inspiration for us all. Listening to these accomplished performers instilled in me the desire to become the best in *my* field, which I hoped would be medicine.

Off campus my pals and I frequently stopped at the Fountainette, known for its triple-dip sundaes and malted milk shakes, and Ma Mary's, home of delicious deep-fried shrimp that was often more batter than shrimp. But who cared? It was always spicy and piping hot!

Famcee had an all-star football team, the Florida Rattlers, and a great marching band that led some outsiders to refer disparagingly to our school as "Florida Athletic and Musical College." Since renamed Florida A&M University, my alma mater was picked by *Time* magazine's *Princeton Review* as "College of the Year" in 1997. At the time I was a student there, it was an all-Negro college and didn't get the credit it deserved for its high academic standards. We students received a traditionalist education and disciplined, top-down teaching, delivered with the expectation that we would listen to our professors and remember what we heard and read. It was an ideal setting for a career in medicine.

Ethan Earl Ware was head of the science department and my premed adviser. He was soft-spoken and masterly, demanding attention to detail, memorization, and organization. Some of my classmates probably could accuse me of joining the Sigma Tau Mu Debating Society to impress Mr. Ware, my adviser, who also served as faculty adviser to the society. I confess it may even have occurred to me that participating in the group's activities was one way to get his attention and show off my gift for memorization, a skill he particularly valued. Nonetheless, the society encouraged public speaking, critical thinking, and logical reasoning, all of which were as valuable to me as actual debating, and I learned nearly as much listening to powerful guest speakers as I did honing my own speaking skills.

Benjamin Mays, president of Atlanta's Morehouse College, impressed me the most. After his riveting address at chapel, he met with a small group of us and someone asked how he could deliver such a superb speech without using any notes. "Speaking from notes is like kissing a beautiful young lady—over the telephone," he replied, with a twinkle in his eye. "The thought is nice, but something is missing!"

Crawford Lindsay of Famcee's English department "spoke" to my other side—the part that loves language and literature. He made learning the rules of grammar fun and could turn a sentence diagram into a thing of beauty. "What is the most common mistake in grammar made by educated people?" Lindsay asked every freshman class. Without waiting for a response, he answered his own question: "The improper use of the nominative for the objective case following a preposition or as a direct object following a transitive verb." If we didn't already know it, we learned to say: "This is just between you and me" instead of you and I, his favorite illustrative example. He emphasized syntax and proper grammar in the written and spoken word. I was exposed to these principles of grammar in high school, but Lindsay made certain that I would remember them.

Famcee students were required to attend chapel six days a week, and Lindsay typically assigned his classes to critique the various speakers who lectured there. The man was a stickler for proper usage, and he often quoted Mark Twain's famous quip that "the difference between the right word and the almost-right word is the difference between lightning and a lightning bug." "Witness the power of lightning!" Lindsay would shout joyously when a student chose just the right word in a classroom presentation. I attribute my passion for proper usage, both my own and that of my students, to Lindsay.

From my college days, I have always had a love for foreign languages. Frances Askew, my college French instructor, made French grammar and its idioms a joy to study. This interest in foreign languages culminated in my studying German years later when I was stationed in Munich for my armed forces tour of duty.

Another professor, Charity Mance, paced the aisles of the psychology lecture hall, probing our psyches to reveal thoughts we didn't know we had. She preached honesty as a core value:

"Often when you first look at truth, she appears ugly," Mance told us, "but the longer you look at her, the more beautiful she becomes." "The prime virtue is courage," she added, "because it makes other virtues possible." She once thrust a clenched fist into the air to illustrate a point about helping others. "If you go through life with a closed hand," she said, "you'll notice that nothing goes out, but nothing comes in, either! You must be willing to *give back*!"

Dr. Russell Anderson, a practicing physician with an M.D. from Howard and a Ph.D. from the University of Pittsburgh, challenged his premed students to apply physiological principles to clinical medicine. One of his examinations required students to "explain the physiological mechanisms in the digestion of a buttered ham sandwich." To answer correctly, of course, you had to know the principles of metabolizing protein, carbohydrate, and fat.

I took my studies seriously, but college opened other worlds as well. Famcee was a college where fraternities were important, and their recruiters worked hard to entice us to join. My most vivid memory of what was called "Alpha Week" is the stentorian voice of Belford F. Lawson Jr., national president of Alpha Phi Alpha and an attorney from Washington, D.C., who inspired me with his call to superior scholarship, responsible leadership, and service to others. I was hooked. In my second semester I became a Sphinxman, as Alpha pledges were called. The next year, after a seemingly interminable initiation process, I "crossed the burning sands" and became a full-fledged "Alpha Man."

Part of our training for full membership in the Beta Nu chapter was learning about Alpha's founding at Cornell University in 1906 as the first black fraternity and especially about its founders—the Seven Jewels—from Brother Charles H. Wesley's *The History of Alpha Phi Alpha—a Development in College Life*. I still know every one of their names: Henry A. Callis, Charles H. Chapman, Eugene Kinckle Jones, George E. Kelly, Nathaniel A.

Murray, Robert H. Ogle, and Vertner M. Tandy—but three of them struck particular chords with me. Callis was a physician and associate professor of medicine at Howard; Chapman served on the faculty at FAMC; and Jones was executive secretary of the National Urban League, one of the nation's most distinguished civil rights groups, from 1918 until 1941.

Perhaps unknowingly, the people who teased us about going to Florida Athletic and Musical College were at least partly correct. One of the most popular singers on campus was William Dandy, who sang like the legendary crooner Billy Eckstine. We had other talented musicians, including Julian and Nat Adderley, who sparked my lifelong love of jazz. Julian, a dear friend and fraternity brother, later won fame as the great "Cannonball" Adderley, master of the alto saxophone. Even in high school, he had been slightly obese and liked to eat, which earned him the nickname "Cannibal." By the time I met him in my freshman year that had somehow evolved into "Cannonball," and the name stuck with him the rest of his life, although some of us shortened it to "Cannon."

My friendship with the Adderleys and their love of jazz lit a fire in me that I later stoked at places such as the Howard Theater in Washington, D.C., and the Apollo Theater and Birdland nightclub in New York City. After leaving Famcee and serving in the Army, Cannonball gained a bit of notoriety in jazz circles when he boldly asked bassist Oscar Pettiford if he could sit in with Pettiford's group while they were playing a gig at Cafe Bohemia in New York City's Greenwich Village in 1955. Curious about this young upstart, Pettiford decided to give him a shot rather than the brush-off. The other members of the band tried to "cut" Cannonball by playing complicated riffs at a rapid pace to show him he was out of his league. Not only could they not cut him, Cannonball's brilliant rendition of "I'll Remember April" was the talk of the town the next day. The entire Village was buzzing about this "bad cat" from Florida who sounded like a combination of Charlie Parker and Benny Carter. He started near the top and kept rising.

Cannonball organized his own quintet with Nat and others but soon left it to join the legendary Miles Davis sextet in 1957. Along with John Coltrane, they recorded the classic Davis jazz album, *Kind of Blue*, in 1959. His memorable saxophone solos on popular cuts from that album, tunes like "So What?" and "Freddie Freeloader," shine as standards of modern jazz today. The following year he left the group to form his own quintet with his brother Nat, had an instant hit with the recording of "Dis Here," and went on to establish himself in jazz legend.

Cannonball, however, had cardiovascular problems, which were complicated by his being overweight. A few months before his death he had a minor stroke. I traveled to New York to visit him in the hospital and found him fully recovered from symptoms of the initial attack. He had no lingering speech or motor problems, but he was frightened, as might be expected. I assured him, speaking as a physician, that he was doing well. Still, he looked deep into my eyes and said, in a tone I've never forgotten, "Yeah, man, I *seem* to be doing well, but suppose I've lost my *soul*? If I've lost *that*, I've lost everything a jazz musician needs to be creative and to *improvise!*"

I sought to reassure him again, this time speaking as a friend, that he had not lost his soul. Indeed, he did recover and went on playing. But it wasn't long after my visit that Julian "Cannonball" Adderley, while performing in Gary, Indiana, suffered a massive stroke and died in August 1975. He was only forty-six years old.

As a college sophomore I joined the staff of the student newspaper, *The Famcean*, and served as editor-in-chief during the summer of 1948. It was a great place to practice writing, and the editorship gave me my first experience as a leader. With the paper's limitations of space, I learned to express thoughts in a concise, cogent manner. I also learned how difficult it can be to get contributing reporters to submit their articles in a timely manner. I honed my people skills trying to get my newspaper staff to work as a team. Those lessons have served me well in leadership positions that I subsequently attained.

In the 1940s the only realistic options for blacks interested in pursuing careers in medicine were Howard University in Washington, D.C., and Meharry Medical College in Nashville, Tennessee. Howard University, named for the Union Civil War hero and Freedmen's Bureau Commissioner General Oliver Otis Howard was founded in 1867, and its medical school was founded the following year. The university was pivotal in providing educational opportunities for the sons and daughters of former slaves. Since its founding, Howard has always admitted white students, but I cannot overemphasize the major role that Howard University, with its various schools and colleges, has played in providing educational opportunities for blacks in this country and abroad. Today black students are accepted, often avidly sought, by all medical schools in this country. In my day, however, there were a number of predominantly white medical schools, but they took almost no blacks. When they did make an exception, it was usually for someone who had excelled at that school's undergraduate level. No white medical schools in the South accepted African-Americans.

During my freshman year, Ralph Wimbish, one of the older students who had returned to college after the war, was accepted to Meharry. Wimbish had taken a liking to me and, unlike most of his Army buddies, never teased me *too* hard. When he got into medical school, he achieved instant superstar status among us premeds. I desperately hoped to duplicate his achievement. My roommate, George Rawls, and I were two of the best students at FAMC, and we both applied to Meharry and Howard for medical school. Yet by spring commencement in 1948, we hadn't heard from either one. My heart was set on going to Meharry because I had friends and a family member who had gone there, and they made it sound wonderful.

It was not to be. Both Rawls and I were rejected. I was greatly disappointed, but knew that if I wanted to achieve my goal I had to continue to study as hard as I could.

I think I failed to get in because, despite my excellent grades, I had only slightly above-average scores on the Professional Aptitude Test, now known as the MCAT (for Medical College Admissions Test). When Dr. William H. Gray Jr., Famcee's president, noted that Rawls and I had not yet heard from Howard's College of Medicine, our only other option, he called his counterpart at Howard, Dr. Mordecai Johnson, who referred him to the dean of the medical school. Gray then made a personal visit to that school's dean, Dr. Joseph L. Johnson, to make a case for admitting us.

Dr. Gray's visit to Howard was unknown to Rawls and me until we heard the good news of our admission to Howard's medical school. I found out in mid-July, while I was still on campus finishing my fast-track bachelor's program. My father drove up to Tallahassee to surprise me, and he had a huge smile on his face. I don't think I'd ever seen him look happier. He spread the letter from Howard on my dorm-room dresser with a flourish.

"It gives me pleasure to advise you that you have been accepted for admission to our September 1948 freshman medical class," the letter began. I'd made it! And as it turned out, Rawls had, too. We quickly agreed to room together in Washington and are still great friends.

My father had already purchased the fifty-dollar money order I needed for the good-faith deposit to hold my place. He had even addressed the envelope. All I had to do was sign the form and drop it in the mail.

Years later, after I'd joined the faculty at Howard's medical school, I asked Dr. Johnson why he had taken a chance on Rawls and me. He said that President Gray had persuaded him that we had the ability to succeed and had demonstrated at Famcee that when exposed to concepts and principles, we could learn it. No one, he had argued, could expect us to excel in subjects we'd

HOWARD UNIVERSITY
WASHINGTON 1, D. C.

OFFICE OF THE REGISTRAR
F. D. WILKINSON

FOUNDED BY GENERAL O. O. HOWARD

July 13, 1948

Mr. LaSalle D. Leffall
P. O. Box 226
Quincy, Florida

Dear Student:

It gives me pleasure to advise you that you have been accepted for admission to our September 1948 freshman medical class pending satisfactory completion of the following on or before September 1, 1948.

1. Results of a personal interview
   --The dean of the medical college will communicate with you in regard to the personal interview.

2. The satisfactory completion of all requirements for admission
   --Please note items checked below, if any.

3. The successful passing of physical and psychometric examination.
   --This examination will be given upon your arrival at the University.

It will be necessary for you to make a good faith deposit of $50.00 on or before ___July 26, 1948___ in order to assure your place. If this deposit is not received on or before the date specified, it will be impossible for us to retain your place. This deposit will be applied to the first installment of your tuition but in the event you subsequently find it impossible to enter, it will not be refunded. All checks and postal money orders should be made payable to Howard University and forwarded directly to the Treasurer of the University.

When we have been notified by the Treasurer that you have made the required payment, when your records are complete in this office showing all requirements have been met, and when we have been advised that your interview has been satisfactory, we will send you a permit to register.

Please fill in the enclosed memorandum and return it to the undersigned.

Very truly yours,

F. D. Wilkinson
Registrar

never taken. On the basis of that argument and President Gray's strong recommendation, Johnson persuaded Howard's medical admissions committee to give us a chance, despite the low standardized test scores.

I think we demonstrated that we were worth the risk. Based on our grades at the end of our sophomore year, Rawls and I were elected vice president and president, respectively, of the Kappa Pi Honor Medical Society (Howard's Alpha Omega Alpha). George went on to become one of the premier surgeons in Indianapolis, Indiana, and although he is now retired, he continues to counsel young people interested in medical careers.

We both know, however, that many students, especially those with public school educations, are even now penalized by their poor grades on standardized tests, for the same reasons that almost prevented George and me from pursuing our dreams. Although the schools these young people attend should be held accountable for teaching them to meet—and beat—both the standards and the odds, students from schools with limited resources should be judged more on how well they have learned what they have actually been taught and not on what others have learned by virtue of greater exposure to good teaching and a better curriculum.

I say: give these students the opportunity, then hold them to the same standards for all students. Lowering standards does a disservice to all, including those to whom I would give the benefit of the doubt, not to mention their patients down the line. But give them a chance—I call it "affirmative opportunity"—and let them prove they can overcome their initial handicap. That's what Rawls and I did.

In September Rawls and I drove to Washington, D.C., with two friends, Monroe Spencer and Lee Royal Hampton, who had been accepted into Howard's dental school. We took Hampton's car, a brand new Packard with its trademark red hexagonal hubs, and we all shared the cost of gasoline. Along the way, we fought good-naturedly about who would get the next chance to drive.

Driving north from Florida required careful planning in those days because it was a two-day trip, and segregation was still the law in the South. We had to make sure that by nightfall we were in a city where one of us knew someone or where there was a black-owned motel or black college to put us up for the night. Young black men of my generation knew well the dangers of being caught in a strange southern town after dark. There were no interstate highways in those days, of course, and only a handful of places between Tallahassee and Washington would take us in. We stopped at Shaw College in Raleigh, North Carolina, then drove on to the capital the next day.

4

Challenge at the Capstone

We arrived in Washington, and Rawls and I checked into George Washington Carver Hall, an off-campus student dorm that cost $40 a month. We hadn't been there long when we spotted a notice on a student bulletin board offering a room not far from campus for half that much. Rawls and I soon moved to 644 Irving Street N.W., the home of Ms. Fannie Dorsey, an elementary school principal who rented rooms to students. The two of us shared a bedroom with twin beds and a two-sided study table. We faced each other across that table and pored over our medical books almost every night for the next four years. The rent was $5 a week. By the time we left in 1952, it had gone up to $7.50. Mrs. Dorsey's was a fifteen-minute walk to the med school, and there was a Chinese restaurant across the street that served bountiful portions for $1.25. I'd never eaten Chinese food before I got to Washington, but I learned to love it. Rawls and I ate there almost every evening.

Seventy-four medical students entered Howard's College of Medicine that September. Dean Johnson, whom we affectionately dubbed "Little Joe," welcomed us warmly, but he let us know we were a privileged few. He told us 1,800 students had applied for the seats we occupied.

I don't think anything can fully prepare a student for medical school. As far as I know, there is no equivalent to having to learn and regurgitate on demand the sheer volume of material we were expected to know, whether it was a broad concept of disease or the Latin name of a microorganism. We simply had to memorize vast amounts of information, then learn how to apply it—on the spot—when a human life might be at stake.

We went to class every weekday from 8 a.m. to noon and from 1 p.m. to 4 p.m. or 5 p.m. We also had class on Saturdays from 8 a.m. to noon. I typically studied six to seven hours after class and ten or twelve hours on Sunday. There were occasional all-nighters, too, of course, but one night a week, either Friday or Saturday, was reserved for fun! We went to the movies, dances, and even had an occasional date, although for me the first three years didn't amount to much socially. I had planned to be a doctor too long to let my guard down and fail, and I'm sure my classmates regarded me as a serious young man on a mission. I tried to go into every examination with confidence that I was so well prepared not a question could stump me. To my dismay, and more often than I care to admit, my professors proved me wrong. But I had a "can-do" attitude and learned I could excel, not just get by. I also had something to prove because of the nature of my acceptance.

Med school demands exceptional discipline, and I soon learned to thrive on it. I've been grateful many times since that I learned to drive myself those first few years because the rigorous training didn't stop then, nor did the demands of practice afterward. The first two years were devoted to the basic sciences, while the last two years were concerned with the clinical sciences. In preparation for our clinical years, med students received lectures in medicine (physical and laboratory diagnoses) and surgery (introduction to surgery) in the latter part of our sophomore year.

Learning the principles shared in these courses and applying them to real life medical problems were essential.

Reflecting on my long career in medicine, I remain grateful for my excellent Howard medical education and training. I will mention briefly my two favorite courses, anatomy and surgery; however, each discipline was important and I learned much from all of them.

Anatomy professor W. Montague Cobb often pounded his students with rapid-fire questions in what we called "bust-out" sessions, and he severely chastised those who got the answers wrong. He was tough, clever, and intolerant of incompetence, and he produced students who were always sharp and ready when challenged. For those who weren't up to it, those bust-out drills were almost a form of abuse. I, however, thrived on them. If you were resolute in your studies, could survive the tirades, and keep up with the pace of Professor Cobb's classes, you could earn a place next to old Imhotep himself, the ancient Egyptian physician who ranked as one of Cobb's greatest heroes.

I actually looked forward to the "cadaver walk," the key component of the final in my Gross Anatomy class. By the end of the term, we students had completely dissected our cadavers, and every identifiable tissue on each was visible somewhere. Dr. Cobb and Dr. Ruth Lloyd, another anatomy professor, would put numbers on any anatomical structure they wished, and we students had to walk around with clipboards and write down the names of each next to the numbers of the various parts. There were 180 items on the list, ranging from muscles to nerves to arteries, veins, bones, parts of the intestinal tract, and any other piece of the human anatomy. We had to know them all cold, without exception. After my first year, and later as a surgical resident, I volunteered to conduct preview classes to help new medical and dental students prepare for the cadaver walk. It was an honor I enjoyed for seven years.

Outside the classroom, Cobb was a leader in the movement to integrate Washington's hospitals, beginning with Gallinger

Municipal Hospital. His widely attended Imhotep conferences, named for that same Egyptian hero of his, were pivotal in breaking down racial barriers throughout Washington's medical community. In 2004, the National Medical Association established the Cobb Health Policy Institute to strengthen the focus on the health problems of ethnic groups and to explore solutions to improve health of all Americans.

The most renowned member of the Howard med faculty was Charles R. Drew, chief of surgery, who, along with his mentor John Scudder at Columbia-Presbyterian Hospital, had done pioneering work on blood preservation. In the fall of 1940 Drew was chosen to head a project to ship plasma to England for use in treating military and civilian casualties. The breakthrough was credited with saving hundreds of lives during the Germans' firebombing of London in World War II. In the spring of 1941 he was named to direct the first American Red Cross blood bank in New York City that supplied blood and plasma to the U.S. Armed Forces after America entered the war. The Armed Forces ruled in 1942 that blood from African-American donors would be accepted but would be stored separately from that of whites. In the controversy that followed, Drew remained above the fray while insisting there was no scientific basis for segregating blood. That policy remained in force until after President Truman ordered desegregation of the Armed Forces in July 1948.

Drew, who had taught at Howard before going to Columbia, had been granted two leaves of absence to pursue his work on the Blood for Britain and American Red Cross projects during the war. Eager to resume his academic career, he returned to Howard in July 1941 as professor and head of the department of surgery.

Students knew him as a singularly dynamic, demanding teacher. I remember one of his oft-repeated sayings that was reminiscent of my father's "no boundaries" speech. "Excellence of performance," Drew said, "will transcend artificial barriers created by man."

I was sitting in Drew's "Introduction to Surgery" lecture on Friday, March 31, 1950, which happened to be the last class he taught. The next day while I was attending a pharmacology lecture, a lab technician walked into the basic science lecture hall and interrupted the talk to whisper something to the professor, Dr. Walter Booker. Booker's face turned ashen, and as he looked back up at us, he solemnly announced that our chief of surgery had been killed that morning in an automobile accident. I looked at the stricken faces of my classmates and wondered how we would survive the loss of such a formidable figure. Class was immediately dismissed, and we wandered from the hall in a daze, deeply saddened.

Drew had been driving with three other physicians to a medical society meeting at Tuskegee Institute in Alabama when their car ran off the road and overturned outside the town of Burlington, North Carolina. His three passengers survived and reported that, despite the best efforts of the medical workers at the local Alamance County hospital, Dr. Drew had succumbed to his injuries a short time after he reached that facility.

The death of one of the nation's most prominent black physicians, perhaps inevitably, spawned rumors in the African-American community that racism in the South was to blame for our loss. Despite his companions' denials, many people chose to believe the story that the famed researcher in preserving human blood had bled to death because the all-white hospital had turned him away. The rumor was perpetuated in October 1964 when one of the nation's most respected civil rights leaders, Whitney M. Young Jr., executive director of the National Urban League, wrote an article entitled "Bigotry and the Blood Bank" published by the *Afro-American* newspapers. Young alleged that Drew had been callously turned away from the nearest hospital, Alamance General, then a whites-only facility, and bled to death "on the way to a nearby 'Negro hospital.'"

"The modern hospital can be the highest expression of compassion, mercy, and love which mankind can present to the world," Young wrote. "It is the duty of every doctor who swears by the Hippocratic Oath to make it so, and to prevent the senseless kind of tragedy which claimed the life of Dr. Charles Drew, whose genius saved the lives of so many others."

My life has been entwined with Drew's name throughout my career, and that story has dogged me incessantly. Having been named professor and chairman of the department of surgery at Howard in July 1970, the same position Drew held from 1941 to 1950, I decided to track down the story to satisfy myself on the question of whether Drew's death did, in fact, have anything to do with his race. The hospital was no longer there, having been replaced by a larger, more modern facility in Burlington, but Marvin Yount, who had been the twenty-nine-year-old administrator at the time, was running the successor Memorial Hospital of Alamance County and was eager to respond to my questions. The local Red Cross had also looked into the case at the request of the National Red Cross a few years before, and a history book, *Eyewitness: The Negro in American History* by William Loren Katz, had claimed Dr. Drew was given plasma at the hospital instead of whole blood because there was only "white" blood on hand.

Yount had attempted to refute the allegation in the interview for the book, insisting that the physician on duty in the emergency room administered plasma "because of Dr. Drew's extreme shock and the speed with which they wanted to get some blood or plasma into him." "In 1950 at the Alamance General we did keep white and black blood labeled separately," Yount acknowledged, "but [we] did not hesitate to interchange when necessary."

The myth, however, refused to die. It was mentioned on the hit television comedy *M.A.S.H.*, a satire set in a military field hospital during the Korean War, and there was talk it would be part of a movie based on Dr. Drew's life.

In April 1983—thirty-three years after the accident—I went to Burlington to see for myself. Yount was still there, and he assembled several people who had treated Drew that day, including the only black man I spoke to about the case, an orderly who remembered helping wheel the injured Drew into the emergency room. They all assured me that no one had turned Drew away or refused him care and that he had received the best care they were able to provide in a small community hospital. They did acknowledge one element of the story that some said proved the charges, however: no hospital record of Dr. Drew's treatment could be found. To me, that was not a cover up but an honest admission. They probably never had time to make a chart in the rush to save his life, and when the failure was uncovered later, they chose not to fabricate the record.

Not long after I returned to Washington, I received a call from Mrs. Lucile Crabtree, a nurse anesthetist, who had been out of town when I visited Alamance General. She said she would be coming to the nation's capital with her son's family in a couple of months and invited me to come to her hotel room at the L'Enfant Plaza to talk about the Drew case. I recall her account with such precision that I feel confident in quoting her.

"I remember it very clearly," she said. "It was Saturday, April 1, 1950. We only ran one operating room on Saturdays, and I had a patient on the table and was getting ready to give him an anesthetic when I was told there had been a major accident out by Haw River and could I come down when the injured came in."

Mrs. Crabtree was told one of the victims was critically injured. "I was so glad I had not given my patient anything yet because if I had, I could not have gone down to the emergency room. I would have been obligated to the patient to whom I've given anesthesia."

She went to the ER and found that of the four people in the car, the only one critically injured was Dr. Drew. One person had a broken arm; the other two had no serious injuries. When she saw Dr. Drew, he was unconscious, and his pupils were dilated, indicating major brain injury. His chest was crushed, and he had an avulsion wound in which the flesh had been torn away from his thigh. His blood pressure was low, he had a rapid pulse, and he was in shock.

"I rapidly put an endotracheal tube in his windpipe to give him oxygen," she said, "and then we started some IV (intravenous) saline solution. We did give plasma but no blood because we didn't have any in our little hospital. By the time it arrived, he was dead. As I recall, he arrived shortly after 8:00 in the morning and was pronounced dead at 10:10, just about two hours later.

"Dr. Leffall, I understand his family has always wondered if he got the proper care and what was actually done. I hope you will tell them from me that I was there from the time he arrived in the emergency room until he died. I put the endotracheal tube in. I gave him oxygen. I monitored his IV fluids. We cared deeply about this man's life and did everything we could."

My knees went weak as I listened to her story in the hotel room, and I was glad I was sitting down. She wasn't bragging; she was looking me straight in the eye and not dodging any responsibility.

Mrs. Crabtree said she had heard stories that they wanted to transfer Drew to another hospital, and those stories were true. "We did want to. Alamance is a small hospital. We thought he would get better care at Duke," the big university hospital in Durham, about thirty miles to the east, where there would be several specialists on staff, "but he died before we could."

I believed her, without question, but the story is still out there. Erroneous accounts of the accident can be found on the Worldwide Web today and in unofficial biographies of Dr. Drew. Several times a year, when third-year Howard medical students take their turn in surgery, I recount the true story of Dr. Drew's demise. I tell my students what a great physician and humanitarian he was, but I also tell them that the myth of his death is untrue.

If we African-Americans let the false story stand to bolster the tragedy of racism, we are just as guilty as we say some whites have been in lying about what happened to us over the years. We must tell the truth, even if it challenges the credibility of a story told by a great civil rights leader or a great black newspaper. If we resort to lying to make a point, we pay too dear a price. I'm not denying, of course, that things like the tale Whitney Young wove have happened, as in the case of the death of the great blues singer Bessie Smith, but the facts never seem to catch up with the myth, and we need to get our facts straight every time.

Jack White, another of my professors of surgery at Howard, often told a story that reveals Charles Drew's inner self. When White was a surgical resident at Freedmen's Hospital, a dirty, unkempt male patient was admitted with a diagnosis of possible intestinal obstruction. In addition to routine laboratory work, the admitting resident ordered abdominal x-rays. A few hours later, Drew was making afternoon rounds with the usual bevy of students, interns, and residents and asked to see the films. The resident informed him that they were still waiting for the transportation service to take the patient to the Radiology Department. Hearing this, Drew, who as always was meticulously attired in his starched white coat, reached into the bed and gathered the patient in his arms. Clutching the patient to his chest, Drew lifted him onto the gurney and wheeled him to the Radiology Suite as his entourage watched in stunned silence. By the time the shame-faced students and young doctors collected their wits, the patient was getting the needed x-rays.

Drew never took the residents to task for their irresponsibility; he didn't have to. The moral force of his example taught them better than any lecture that a physician is never too busy or too important to help a patient.

During the summers of 1950 and 1951, a medical school classmate, Freddie McFadden, and I worked at the Sankaty Head Golf

Club on Nantucket Island in Massachusetts. Freddie's father was the head Red Cap at Grand Central Station in the days when baggage handlers were known by their distinctive red headgear, and he had learned about the openings at the club from a businessman he had served. Freddie was the main bartender, and I worked as a waiter and occasionally tended bar. The club was hectic on weekends, but things were slower during the week, and in down times Freddie and I discovered that if we left a medical book on a corner of the bar, club members couldn't help but notice and would invariably ask us about it. We, of course, used the prop to ease into a conversation about how we were working our way through medical school. The gambit often netted us larger tips, and while I suspect several of the club members recognized our little hustle, they figured they were donating to a good cause.

One member with whom I chatted on numerous occasions was Walter Beinecke, a successful businessman whose family donated the funds to underwrite the Beinecke Rare Book Library at Yale University and to rebuild the historic wharves once used by the Nantucket whaling fleet. Beinecke spoke movingly about his family, telling stories to show how his own father had taught his sons the importance of teamwork and giving back to the community. I recall one tale he shared in which his father gave one of his sons a pony, another a cart, and the third a bridle and harness, then told each of them to bring him back some particular item from town. The boys figured out they would have to combine their assets and work together if they were to get to town and do as their father asked. The three brothers—Edwin, Frederick, and Walter—later founded the Sperry and Hutchinson Co., which produced S&H Green Stamps, a national retailing fixture that led to modern-day discount programs like airline frequent-flyer miles.

After my second summer on Nantucket I went home to Quincy before returning to school. My father came down to the train station to meet me. I was shocked when I saw him. I knew he had been ill for several months with high blood pressure, and while I was in Nantucket he had been hospitalized. But when I spotted him as I stepped off the train, I instantly realized that the once-stocky six-footer had lost a tremendous amount of weight. As long as I had known him, he had always worn his belt buckled at the first hole. Now it was cinched up three or four notches with the loose end dangling aimlessly.

I wanted to cry. I didn't have to be in medical school to know he was a very sick man. His blood pressure was uncontrolled, despite the best treatment available and his weeks in the FAMC hospital. He had been to some of the best doctors in Tallahassee, but there were only a couple of medications available in those days to treat his condition, and he wasn't responding.

Mother asked me during that visit if I thought he would recover. I had to tell her it was unlikely he would get a lot better. But my father was insistent that I return to Washington for my last year of medical school. "Your mother, sister, and I will be up next summer" for graduation, he said. "All of us are planning to be there in June." He never gave me any indication he didn't expect to make it. I left for Washington a few days later.

Barely a month passed before my mother telephoned to tell me, "Daddy's had a stroke. We had to take him to the hospital." I rushed to the dean's office to get permission to leave school, but my father died before I could get home to see him.

It was October 8, 1951. He was just fifty-one years old. I went back for the funeral and spent a few days with my mother and sister, but Mother insisted that I not lose any more time away from my studies and reminded me that my father would have wanted more than anything else for me to finish the year and go on with my life.

Back at school, I realized the tuition for my final year had not been paid, and I thought I would have to find a job. Up to that point, my parents had paid all my expenses to enable me to devote full time to my studies during the school year. My father had been adamant that I not give up study time as long as he could provide my support. Now, he wasn't there to help, and I knew that taking a job might force me to delay graduation or, worse, to give up my dream.

Recalling my conversations with Walter Beinecke that summer, I wrote to him and told him of my family's loss. I explained my desperate financial straits and asked him for a loan of five hundred dollars to pay my tuition and fees. I promised to repay him as soon as I was able.

Beinecke replied within days, enclosing a check for the amount I had requested and a letter telling me it was not a loan but a gift—with two stipulations: that I do the same for some other deserving student someday; and that I become a worthy, caring physician. In the years to come, I did help needy students financially on occasion, always remembering my pledge to Beinecke. In 1997, thanks to some fortunate investments, I was able to give $350,000 to my alma mater, then known as Florida A&M University, to be used for scholarships. The only conditions I set were that the grants be made without regard to gender, race, or religion. Under a state matching fund program, the school actually received $525,000 and set up an endowment fund in memory of my parents.

As for Beinecke's second condition, to this day I consciously try to care for each of my patients and be worthy of their trust each and every day. Of course, I wrote Beinecke to thank him for his kindness, and we corresponded several times after that, but I never saw him again. He died of cancer in 1958.

Almost a half century after that summer on Nantucket I met his daughter, Betsy Shirley, and told her the story of how her father had helped me and what I had done to fulfill his terms. It was a touching—and tearful—moment for both of us.

I've only been back to the Sankaty Head Golf Club once. When a friend of mine, Walter "Derby" Wilson, was president of the club in 2002, he invited me to visit as a guest of the club. It brought back fond memories. It didn't seem to have changed all that much either. I wondered if they still have young medical students mixing drinks—and whether those students leave their books on the bar to enhance their tips.

During my first three years in medical school, I had occasional dates but nothing serious—until a friend in the dean's office, Margaret "Mikey" McWilliams, insisted on introducing me to her younger sister Ruthie. Ruthie was working as a secretary at Freedmen's Hospital, the teaching hospital for Howard University's medical school. Her family was from Richmond, and she had recently graduated from Virginia Union University in her hometown with a degree in history. She had come to Washington to live with her sister and attend graduate school.

Mikey had me over for dinner, and I was smitten the moment I walked in the door. Not only was Ruthie pretty and stylish, I quickly learned she was also intelligent, challenging, and had a completely disarming sense of humor. For me, at least, it was love at first sight.

I invited her to the annual Med-Dent Ball, the highlight of the social season for Howard's medical and dental students, and I puffed up with pride when I walked in with her on my arm. Duke Ellington, a native Washingtonian, was leading his orchestra that night, and I thought Ruthie was the very embodiment of the Duke's "Sophisticated Lady." That tune has been my favorite Ellington song ever since.

In June 1952, Ruthie sat with my mother during Honors and Oath Day as my class members and I took the Hippocratic Oath for the first time. I have repeated it almost every year since when physicians in the audience are asked to join the new doctors of medicine in pledging "to follow that method of treatment which, according to my ability and judgment, I consider for the benefit of my patients and abstain from whatever is deleterious and mischievous."[1] As I basked in the glow of my mother's joy and my

---

[1] From a modern version composed by members of the Howard University College of Medicine Class of 1972.

beloved Ruthie's affection, I vowed privately to live by the oath I had just taken and felt deeply the gravity of the responsibility I was about to shoulder. Call it corny, but I believed I was making a solemn pact with my patients, and I feel that bond just as strongly now as I did that day.

I was honored to be named first in my class of newly minted MD's and first in surgery, medicine, and obstetrics-gynecology. It was a heady time, a beautiful clear day, and President Truman was about to give the commencement address, but it was a bittersweet triumph for me. No one had wanted to witness that ceremony more than my father did. No one would have been prouder. That evening, as Mother, Dolores, Ruthie and I celebrated my twenty-second birthday, which had occurred some three weeks before, we observed a moment of silence in his memory.

For all the emphasis my medical training had placed on science, reason, and the importance of scrutinizing clinical evidence, I could nonetheless feel my father's presence at the ceremonies that day. I could almost see him sitting in the audience, right there next to my mother and Ruthie, showering me with approving looks and silent praise. My joy was his joy at that moment, and his joy mine.

5

Missouri to Manhattan:
My Training Continues

The winter of my senior year, I started thinking about where to apply for my internship, a year-long introduction to all the major fields of medicine. In some ways, Freedmen's Hospital in Washington was an obvious choice. As the teaching hospital for Howard University, it was already familiar ground, and, of course, I would be near Ruthie. But in talking to earlier graduates and to my advisers, I was inclined to look at other hospitals. I had informal assurances that I could return to Freedmen's for my residency, and it seemed the right time for a different challenge. I wanted to look at my new profession from a fresh point of view. I told Ruthie and my friends that I planned to go away for that year to get a flavor of elsewhere.

There were at the time three other black teaching hospitals that beckoned—Harlem Hospital in New York City; Hubbard Hospital, attached to Meharry Medical College in Nashville; and Homer G. Phillips Hospital in St. Louis. I was also thinking, probably for the first time seriously, of trying to step out of the familiar world of black education to seek an appointment in a predominantly white hospital. I knew my Howard medical education was first-rate, and I had graduated at the top of my class. I figured I could handle whatever was thrown at me, and I was pretty sure that if a white hospital decided to take me, they would want me to succeed.

In talking to graduates from the previous year who had just been through the process, I learned about the excellent training being offered at Detroit Receiving Hospital, and I decided that that site would be a great choice. Even though it was in the North, I was told, Detroit Receiving took whites almost exclusively and usually students from Wayne State or one of the other medical schools in that region. That wasn't a particularly daunting prospect for me, however, because I really wanted to test myself. I knew I had the dedication and drive, and it never crossed my mind that I wouldn't measure up. As my experience at Howard had shown me, if given a chance I could succeed. So I applied there anyway. With my class ranking and credentials, I just knew I would beat the odds.

No such luck. It was 1952, and there just weren't many black doctors accepted for postgraduate training at the nation's major teaching hospitals. Fortunately, I also applied to Homer G. Phillips Hospital in St. Louis and was accepted there. I was disappointed about not being accepted at Detroit Receiving, but I didn't dwell on it. As my father used to say, quoting a well-worn phrase, "The measure of a man's real character is how he responds in the face of adversity." My response was to accept my fate and move on.

I won't say that I just shrugged it off, but I wasn't bitter, either. I told myself: "Okay, I'll go to Phillips, and someday they'll know in Detroit that they made a mistake." If anything, the rejection strengthened my resolve to do my job so well, wherever I went, that *I* would know they made a mistake by not taking me. I was also reasonably confident that the negative decision wasn't personal, and I tried not to take it that way, but I was pretty sure not all their interns were first in their classes.

Going to St. Louis turned out to be fortuitous. There were few white hospitals in the country that provided the range of experiences I had at Phillips—a big, busy, inner-city hospital that was the only choice for most blacks in that city. Residents there saw all kinds of diseases: cancer, heart disease, stroke, kidney failure—you name it—and plenty of trauma, too, including gunshot wounds, stabbings, accidents of all kinds. Many white hospitals had the diseases but not the trauma. Others had the trauma but sent their serious diseases elsewhere. At Phillips we got it all.

It's funny how things work out. I'd wanted to attend Meharry but was rejected there and later accepted at Howard. I'd wanted to do my internship at Detroit Receiving, but was turned away and ended up at Phillips in St. Louis. Both initial disappointments turned out to be major turning points in my life. Then, as now, I learned the truth of the adage: It's not the hand you're dealt that matters, but how you play it. I also believe that I was led—by some divine, intervening force—not away from what I had wanted but toward what turned out to be best for me. I later developed close relationships with both institutions that earlier denied me, but I spent most of my career at Howard, and a return trip to Phillips years later led to a major breakthrough in my professional life.

Interning, now called first-year residency, is the freshly minted doctor's introduction to handling real-world situations without another physician present, although interns are always supervised by attending physicians. On my first night on duty in the emergency room at Phillips, a seventy-three-year-old farmer came in complaining of abdominal pain, nausea, and vomiting. No problem; I vividly recalled Dr. Burke Syphax's lectures at Howard on the acute abdomen and proceeded to gather the necessary information for a diagnosis. As I examined the patient, however, I didn't get the answers I was looking for. I asked one probing question after the other, trying to isolate his pain and determine its cause, but the farmer just responded with a series of blank stares and shoulder shrugs. I went down my mental list, ruling out appendicitis, inflammation of the gall bladder, pancreatitis, perforated peptic ulcer, perforated colon cancer. Nothing I knew seemed to apply to his symptoms. I couldn't figure out what was wrong with the man.

I thought to myself: "Oh, no, I'm going to fail to make the correct diagnosis my very first night in the ER!" Then I recalled that there are two diagnoses physicians never make: one about a disease they don't know about and the other about diseases they don't think about. Nearly exasperated, I asked my patient one more time if anything unusual had happened to him recently. At that moment, his wife walked into the examining room. She overheard my question to her husband and said to him, "What about that bite you told me about yesterday?"

"What bite?" I asked. The old farmer waved his hand dismissively and said to his wife, "Oh that was just an ol' black widow spider, woman! That's *nothing!*"

I could feel the smile creep across my face. The abdominal pain of a bite by a black widow spider, I had learned in med school, mimics pancreatitis or ulcer. I immediately knew that I was dealing with one of the nonsurgical causes of acute abdomenal pain. I gave the patient some calcium gluconate, analgesics, and intravenous fluids, and we had him fixed up in no time.

I'm still reminded of that incident when I see a less-than-obvious case that reinforces my determination never to rule out exceptional circumstances when making a diagnosis.

There were also times at Phillips when my colleagues and I were on the leading edge of patient care, a point of pride I often recalled during my twelve months in St. Louis. Dr. Carl Moyer was the Bixby professor and chairman of surgery at Washington University in St. Louis and one of the leading surgical physiologists in the world. He had written *Fluid Balance*, the "bible" on abnormalities of the body's fluids and electrolytes, and we residents had to learn everything in it. And believe me, we did, too.

Moyer came over once a month to conduct grand rounds, and on one occasion, he announced that residents would be the first to get some momentous medical news. His research team had just completed a study on the use of silver nitrate to treat burns. Although the chemical made an awful mess—staining bed linens, surgical gowns, and everything it touched an ugly brown—the Moyer study determined that when applied to severe burns, silver nitrate caused wounds to heal more quickly, helped prevent infection, and enabled patients to be discharged from the hospital sooner than when they were treated with the standard medicines at that time. Moyer told us the findings were just in, but he said, "I'm giving you this report even before I report to the faculty at Barnes Hospital," the teaching hospital for Washington University Medical School, his home turf. At Phillips, where we had a number of burn cases and a very busy trauma center, this was information we could put to good use right away.

Fortunately, particularly from nurses' point of view, medical science has moved on since then. Silver nitrate has been replaced by less unsightly treatments because the people who had to handle the stuff hated it. But it was great to be at the forefront of medical knowledge.

It was also at Phillips that I first heard a lecture by Dr. Matthew Walker, Chief of Surgery at Meharry. I had heard so many laudatory comments about Dr. Walker from my fellow interns who were Meharry graduates. He spoke on "Pre- and Post-Operative Care of the Surgical Patient," emphasizing the pathophysiology of the cardiopulmonary and renal systems. Later, while I was serving as chair of the surgery department at Howard, I invited Dr. Walker to be a visiting professor there. On both occasions he lived up to his stellar reputation. In 1982 surgical department chair Dr. Louis Bernard invited me to Meharry to give the Hale-McMillan Lecture, which was begun by Dr. Walker in 1948.

One of my first impressions of Phillips had been formed

even before I got there. It was a tradition at Howard that a physician who had graduated twenty years before would be selected to return to speak at Honors and Oath Day. The twenty-year alumnus in my graduating year was Dr. William Sinkler of Phillips Hospital. His address emphasized treating patients with respect, but it was not until I worked in St. Louis that I got some first-hand experience in what he meant. I was attending the weekly morbidity and mortality conference in which Phillips residents reviewed their toughest cases with the hospital's attending surgeons to discuss how to improve treatment the next time something similar presented itself. One of the residents was presenting his case and referred to his patient by her first name without calling her Miss or Mrs. (This was before the courtesy title "Ms." was adopted.) Dr. Sinkler interrupted the presentation and told the resident, "As long as you are here, don't ever call an adult man or woman by his or her name without Mr., Miss, or Mrs." He turned to us and added, "I hope I've made a point to all of you. Always treat your patients with respect and dignity."

It's a little thing, perhaps, but little things can be important.

Even before I left Howard for Homer Phillips, I had decided to pursue surgery as my specialty. Listening to lectures by Dr. Drew and Associate Professor of Surgery Burke "Mickey" Syphax had planted that seed. From their example I learned to think of surgery as the only path for me to follow. All other disciplines paled in comparison.

It was not only the influence of my mentors that guided me. I grew up loving precision and big challenges. Surgery requires exactitude, decisiveness, and efficiency, all qualities I cultivated in medical school. I also liked the problem-solving nature of the discipline and the ability to provide quick, dramatic relief to patients. A surgeon takes care of things and doesn't drag out the cure. Bad appendix? Take it out. Bad gall bladder? Remove it. Of course, there are combination treatments, but generally a surgeon and his patient don't have to wait years—except in some cancer cases—to know if the treatment's going to work.

After my year of internship, rotating through all the major services—medicine, surgery, OB/Gyn, pediatrics, and psychiatry—I returned to Washington in July 1953 to begin my surgical residency at Freedmen's Hospital. It was good to be back in the District of Columbia, to renew old friendships and to visit many of the national monuments and historical sites that I had been too busy to enjoy as a medical student. It was also wonderful to be with Ruthie again. She had come to visit me during that year in St. Louis, but it had been lonely without her.

Soon after my return I was assigned my first operation, the rite of passage for a surgical resident. It was an appendectomy, and Dr. Bernard "Gip" Gipson, a surgery instructor who had just finished his own residency and wasn't that much older than I was, was to guide me through it. Of course, I'd read extensively about the proposed procedure and the proper surgical technique, and I was primed to get on with it. I scrubbed meticulously and ceremoniously donned my gown and gloves in the operating room.

As I stood over the patient, I asked the nurse to pass me the scalpel and I began to cut. Slowly, I made a right lower-quadrant transverse incision into the patient's abdomen. Too slowly. After an agonizing few moments of silence, Gip let go: "Leffall! You don't have to see cells in mitosis [dividing] before you cut through the tissue! If you don't get a move on, the incision will have healed before you get to the appendix! Cut! *Cut!*"

I could hear the muffled laughter coming from behind the surgical masks of my colleagues in the operating room and was momentarily taken aback. But Gip's wry humor broke the tension, and I relaxed. My characteristic confidence returned, and I proceeded to do what I believe I was born to do. The abdomen opened under my knife, and I had the appendix out in no time. The patient was soon on the way to recovery.

That year I did rotations in anesthesiology, neurosurgery and general surgery before getting another chance to cross the color line. Washington, D.C., had a second predominantly black inner-city hospital in those days known as Gallinger Municipal. It was a large public hospital with more than 1,200 beds and was considered an excellent facility for postgraduate medical training because, like Phillips in St. Louis and similar big-city hospitals, it dealt with large numbers of patients with a wide variety of problems. Although Gallinger served mostly black patients, it was run by whites. The medical schools at Georgetown and George Washington universities controlled all the services and used Gallinger to supplement their own teaching hospitals on campus. It was a wonderful teaching environment, but Howard University, which was physically closer than either of the other two schools, wasn't part of it.

One of Dr. Drew's goals was to get a spot at Gallinger for a surgical resident from Howard. He approached his counterpart at Georgetown, Dr. Robert Coffey, with a proposal to rotate Howard residents through the service at Gallinger, and in 1950, Georgetown accepted its first surgical resident from Howard into its Gallinger service. Four years later, I became the fourth of those residents.[2] As the only black surgical resident at Gallinger, I could have been an easy target. Washington and medicine were both still segregated in the mid-1950s, and prejudice could have made my life difficult. Dr. Coffey was determined not to let that happen. Coffey and Drew had an excellent working relationship built on mutual respect, and after Drew was killed in the car crash in 1950, Coffey kept the Howard Gallinger program going. He told his residents the experiment simply had to work, and they accepted his word as fact.

I was confident of my abilities, but I suppose it was only natural for me to wonder how I'd measure up against my white

---

[2] Gallinger, which was later renamed D.C. General Hospital, granted the Howard University College of Medicine its own surgical residency program in 1958.

fellow residents. With the power of Coffey's personality, however, I felt I was immediately part of the team at Gallinger, not an appendage or an unwelcome presence.

I soon had occasion to win my spurs. Not long after my arrival, the noted Georgetown cardiovascular surgeon, Dr. Charles Hufnagel, came to perform an operation at Gallinger, and I was among a group of residents selected to assist him. Hufnagel was in a good mood, humming and lightly singing a catchy little song as he worked. "*Clonorchis sinensis, Clonorchis sinensis!*" he sang happily, until unexpectedly he turned to us residents and asked, "What's *Clonorchis sinensis*?" Coincidentally, I had given a report on that obscure organism in a parasitology class in medical school, so I knew what it was.

"It's a Chinese liver fluke," I said.

A hush fell over my colleagues around me. My colleagues at Gallinger viewed me in a whole new light after that! It was largely good luck, actually. There were many, many parasites I knew nothing about, but Dr. Hufnagel had just happened to be crooning about one I knew.

When my year at Gallinger was up, I returned to Freedmen's Hospital to complete my final two years of residency, receiving most of my clinical training under Drs. Burke Syphax and Jack White. Syphax was known as the "Master of the Abdomen" because he had superb diagnostic and technical skills in that area of the body. He always stressed the importance of studying a patient's medical history, conducting a thorough physical examination, and correlating the two. He earned the respect of radiologists for his keen eye in interpreting abdominal x-rays, often picking up subtleties that less-skilled doctors missed. No one had better surgical judgment, that vital combination of knowledge, intelligence, experience, analysis—and restraint.

A great surgeon knows when *not* to operate. Syphax was a stickler for proper surgical technique: how to hold the scalpel, how to make an incision, how to dissect tissue, and how to suture the tissue gently and precisely. Except under special circumstances, which he carefully explained, the scalpel must be held at a right angle to the tissue being cut or the incision will be beveled and may not heal properly. He also taught us to select the right needle for each procedure and to pick a suture size just large enough to hold and small enough not to interfere with healing.

After Dr. Drew's untimely death, Syphax became chief of general surgery with responsibility for training surgical residents. He later was named professor and chair of the department. He stepped into the shoes of a charismatic—even heroic—figure in medicine and succeeded despite the inevitable comparisons to the revered figure who had preceded him. Although he generously relinquished the position to me some years later when he had several years before retirement, Mickey Syphax remained a full member of the faculty from 1940 to 2001, a career spanning a remarkable sixty-one years.

Jack White had been the first black doctor accepted for a cancer fellowship at Memorial Sloan-Kettering Cancer Center in New York in 1949, and it was his enthusiasm for using the advanced surgical techniques he learned there that persuaded me to pursue a career in cancer surgery. White taught Freedmen's residents how to perform procedures such as radical neck dissection for people with mouth or throat cancer that had spread to their lymph nodes in the neck. The operation sometimes involved disfiguring surgery, but it offered the possibility of survival and improved quality of life for patients who otherwise had little chance. I adopted it not just because it was an advanced technical procedure but also because it could enable people to return to society as productive citizens. We also learned about major stomach, pancreatic, and liver resections—life-altering techniques, to be sure—used in cases of advanced cancer when there is no other possible cure. Before these radical methods were developed, people with such tumors just died miserable deaths. The procedures change body image and function, but with appropriate reconstruction and psychological

61

support, patients who undergo them can recover and lead productive lives. From Dr. White I learned the great satisfaction of taking some risks, knowing I could give my patients the fighting chance they would not have if I failed to act boldly. In my early years at Freedmen's, however, my steps were measured ones, and I had lots to absorb.

As residents, we all lived at the Freedmen's Interns Home next to the hospital. The quarters were spartan, with only a bed, desk, closet, and a phone for each resident, but we worked long hours and spent many sleepless nights in the hospital. Living close together fostered a camaraderie that made friends for life. As a budding surgeon, I kept a string tied around my bedpost to practice tying knots. Every night when I got back to my room, I spent some time tying square knots and surgical knots until I could make them with a fluid, one-handed motion. It's a point of pride with surgeons to get the knots just right, to make sure they don't slip—and to look good while doing it. I also had a suture board in my room with a pliers-like needle holder and needle to practice holding the tools properly while sewing up a wound.

Residents' social lives were governed by the "Dollar Club," an informal arrangement that financed parties, TV sports events, and movies by assessing each resident $1 for refreshments. Our financial straits dictated that beer, not the hard stuff, was the beverage of choice. Okay, it wasn't the wildest life in town, but we worked hard and had some fun, too.

Outside the Interns' Home were two benches that served a vital role in the bonding and maturation of young doctors at Howard. Almost every afternoon when residents and interns got off duty, we gathered at those benches and compared notes about the day. It was there we struggled with the tough, emotional part of holding others' lives in our hands. We often worked with very sick patients, and we knew we couldn't win them all. The benches were our place to bare our souls; to vent, seek reassurance, and know that we had the support and understanding of others who were going through the same trials.

I had one elderly patient on whom I operated for intestinal obstruction. She didn't get better for a long time, and I struggled with that day after day. There were formal occasions to discuss the technicalities of her case with the attending surgeons at the hospital, of course, but at the benches, my fellow residents listened to me describe how the case was going. They heard and felt my anxiety at not knowing what else to do. They offered encouragement, made suggestions, and assured me that I was doing everything anyone could. With their support, I grew more comfortable with my decisions and confident of my actions. My patient did eventually recover, but the camaraderie of my colleagues at the benches made me stronger.

During all these years, Ruthie had waited patiently while I prepared for my career. We had met my senior year in medical school, and she had tolerated our long separations during my year in St. Louis, then three more years of residency. On Valentine's Day, 1956, I took the inevitable next step. I picked her up at Lucy Diggs Slowe Hall, where many of the young ladies who were working at Howard or in downtown Washington lived, and I took her out to dinner to ask if she would marry me.

I hadn't bought a ring yet. I was earning more than the $50 a month I made as an intern at Phillips, but even surgical residents had a tough time getting by. My salary then was less than $250 a month. But either Ruthie didn't care or she figured my prospects were pretty good because she accepted on the spot. She insisted, however, that I write to ask her father for her hand, and he wrote back saying the family would be honored to have me as a son-in-law. Then and later, I realized that my future in-laws were the best kind any man could hope to have: supportive and non-intrusive.

A group of my close friends threw a bachelor party for me at the Interns' Home. It was a wild party by Dollar Club standards. I think they broke the bank when they brought in the belly dancer!

63

Ruthie and I were married in Andrew Rankin Chapel on the Howard campus on August 18, 1956. Washington can be unbearably hot in August, and our wedding day was no exception. Despite the sultry atmosphere, Ruthie was magnificent in her white gown and the guests, dressed up in pretty summer outfits, seemed to enjoy themselves. Our honeymoon on Martha's Vineyard gave us a few days far away from my hectic life as a resident to begin a marriage that continues to grow stronger through love and mutual respect.

I had only one year to go to finish my residency, then I was scheduled to report for military duty. It was shortly after the Korean War, and all the nation's young men faced the prospect of being drafted, but doctors were a special case. Draft-age men, that is, those between eighteen and twenty-six, could be expected to be called up sometime in their early twenties and serve at least two years in the enlisted ranks of the Army unless they flunked the physical, volunteered for longer tours to get better duty, or were deferred for college or graduate school. Those who weren't called by the time they were twenty-six were exempt—unless they were studying medicine or dentistry. Because the military always needs skilled physicians, surgeons, and dentists, we were granted as many deferments as we needed to become fully qualified specialists and were assured of being commissioned as officers in the Medical Corps. But we had to report to serve our two-year obligation as soon as we completed residency, no matter how old we were.

I was scheduled to finish my surgical residency in 1957, and the Army was expecting me to report soon afterward. However, in my final year of training I was offered a two-and-a-half-year senior surgical oncology fellowship at Memorial Hospital for the Treatment of Cancer and Allied Diseases, known today as Memorial Sloan-Kettering Cancer Center. It was the premier institution of its kind in the world and an honor and opportunity I couldn't possibly pass up. Jack White, my surgery professor, had been accepted there, thanks to the recommendation of Dr. Drew. White had encouraged me to apply and gave me his full support. One other black physician, a fellow from Meharry, had followed White, and a couple others had served one-year appointments. I would be the third member of my race to be named a senior fellow.

My reaction to my acceptance at Sloan-Kettering was comparable to that day in July 1948 when my father brought me the news I had been admitted to medical school. I was bursting with pride as I told Ruthie, and once more I was reminded of my father's words: "With a good education and hard work, combined with honesty and integrity, there are no boundaries."

I wrote to the Army and practically begged to be allowed to accept this once-in-a-lifetime opportunity. With the assistance and support of the late Congressman Adam Clayton Powell III, I obtained an affirmative reply, but on condition that I agree to enter the Armed Forces as soon as my fellowship was over. Ruthie and I left Washington for New York City in late June 1957.

It wasn't that I was crossing the historic color line and entering a predominantly white institution. I won't deny that I noticed, and, of course, that was a formidable factor. But unlike my decision to apply unsuccessfully to Detroit Receiving for an internship five years earlier, seeking admission to Memorial was more than just going north to a big-city hospital. As White had told me time and again from his own experience, Memorial Sloan-Kettering was the most exciting place in the world to learn and practice cancer surgery. Patients whose cases were considered hopeless anywhere else were simply viewed as another challenge there. Cancer surgery and cardiac surgery were the hottest areas of the specialty at that time, and Sloan-Kettering was *the* place for cancer research, treatment, innovation, combined therapies, and the search for cures to the most perplexing cases. I was thrilled at the prospect of working with and learning from outstanding cancer specialists. I would be on the cutting edge, working with the best—including Chief of Surgery Dr. Henry "Tom" Randall, a leading surgical physiologist—and my new colleagues and members of the staff would quickly become my mentors, advisers, and friends.

I expected the hospital, given its dedication to serving people with advanced disease, to be a sullen, morose institution, and I prepared myself for a tough life in the cancer wards. Instead, I found it to be a warm and cheerful place that exuded dignity, compassion, and hope. The hospital's welcoming committee threw a lively party to celebrate the arrival of the new fellows, and I felt immediately at ease in my new environment.

Ruthie and I were assigned an apartment in the newly constructed Phipps House for surgical residents, just across the street from the hospital at 445 East 68th Street between First and York avenues. Our apartment, spacious by New York standards, had a living room, bedroom, bathroom, kitchen, and small dining area. It rented for $100 a month, which was taken directly out of my pay (the hospital provided a substantial rent subsidy). It was a tremendous bargain. Once a week, spouses were allowed to join us for a free meal at the hospital's special cafeteria for attending and house staff. Ruthie and I usually picked the day they served lobster.

Ruthie quickly found a job preparing educational materials for IBM, and we set out to enjoy our time in New York City. After the rent and food, we had about $200 a month to live on, which wasn't a lot, but with Ruthie's salary, our income covered our other expenses, tickets to movies at the 68th Street Playhouse, and gas for my prized possession: a 1956 turquoise-and-cream Chevy Bel Air that I had bought when I was chief resident at Freedmen's.

We were also fortunate that many of the attending physicians at Memorial invited us to their homes for dinner frequently. They also offered us theater tickets if they were unable to use them. We saw quite a few Broadway productions that way, went to the opera and symphony, and lived much better than our limited budget would otherwise have allowed.

Ruthie and I also visited the Museum of Modern Art, the Metropolitan Museum of Art, and the Frick and numerous galleries, trying to take full advantage of what we knew was a limited stay in the "city that never sleeps." Both she and I share an insatiable desire to learn more about everything we can— especially literature, music, and art. This quest for knowledge I'm sure goes back to our early childhoods and something fostered by our parents and teachers.

Back at the hospital, though, the lessons weren't always easy. One of my first assignments at Sloan-Kettering was serving as chief resident for its Gastric and Mixed Tumor Service. Dr. Gordon McNeer, the associate chief of the service at that time, once kept on me for several days, reminding me to be sure that the clinic would be covered by a resident on a particular day because the operating schedule that day was going to be particularly heavy and all the other residents would be busy. I assured him that I would take care of it and assigned the task to one of the junior residents.

On the day in question, I was in the operating room when I received an emergency page that McNeer wanted to see me immediately. I "broke scrub," leaving the OR and letting the other surgeons finish the procedure. When I arrived at the service office, McNeer was waiting for me. He demanded to know why the clinic was not being covered. I was dumbfounded, but before I could respond, he bellowed, "I don't want *any* excuses! I told *you* to make sure that the clinic was covered! It *wasn't!*"

I stood there, my mind struggling to understand what had happened when I thought I had made sure we were covered. I quickly realized, however, that regardless of what had happened, I had to take the blame. Mustering all my inner strength to maintain my equanimity, I told McNeer I would go to the clinic myself immediately and would take steps to ensure that no such lapse would occur again.

After clinic hours were over, I met privately with the junior resident who had left his post and gave him a second-hand version of the same chewing out that McNeer had given me.

That incident emphasized the importance of accepting responsibility for a task to its completion. It also taught me that the only proper response when called on the carpet is to apologize for the failure, try to correct the problem, and pledge to prevent a recurrence. Above all, I learned, don't give excuses!

I was angry and upset by McNeer's biting words and strident tone, but I believe he treated me as he would have treated any other resident who had failed to complete an assigned task. He wasn't picking on me because I was black, nor did he go easy on me for that reason. The more I thought about the incident, the more I appreciate it for having taught me a most valuable lesson.

Other lessons weren't always so personal. While I was serving as chief resident for Dr. Alexander Brunschwig's Gynecological Service at Sloan-Kettering, a wealthy white woman from the South was admitted to the hospital with advanced cancer of the uterus that had spread to both her bladder and rectum. She needed an operation that we called total pelvic exenteration, which involves removal of the bladder, uterus, and rectum, and the creation of an artificial bladder and a permanent colostomy for the elimination of body waste. At that time, few surgeons would perform such a procedure. Brunschwig had popularized the use of this radical surgery for advanced gynecological malignancies and was probably the best-known surgeon for this particular procedure. Given the advanced stage of her disease, he was this patient's last hope.

I went to examine the patient but she refused, stating fervidly that she would allow only a white physician to perform the examination. Dr. Brunschwig was informed of this, and when he and I visited her room for afternoon rounds, he shocked her—and me—by telling her, in a calm and dispassionate tone. that she was being discharged. Startled and perplexed, the patient reminded him that she was scheduled for an operation the following day. Without batting an eye, he coolly explained that he had been informed that she had refused to allow the assigned resident to examine her and that her action was grounds for her discharge.

Tears began streaming down the woman's cheeks. Although she was in desperately frail condition, she climbed out of her bed and grabbed Dr. Brunschwig by the lapels of his lab coat.

"Please!" she pleaded. "Don't send me home! You're my last hope!"

With steely-eyed composure, Brunschwig eased the distraught patient back onto her bed and told her, "I'll keep you in the hospital and operate tomorrow. But I *never* want to hear again that you refused to allow any person on my team to perform his duties! Is that understood?"

"Yes," she replied, in her newfound humility.

The next morning, the woman underwent the radical resection Brunschwig had made famous. During her long postoperative stay at Sloan-Kettering, I came to know her quite well, and we established a close rapport, as doctor and patient should. One day, as we were chatting, she confessed to me, "Dr. Leffall, prejudice can be a terrible thing. As an adult, I should know better, but that's how I was reared." She eventually went home, free of cancer.

Years later, when Nobel Laureate Elie Wiesel asked me to participate in a conference called "The Anatomy of Hate" in Oslo, Norway, in 1990, I cited this case as an example of how prejudice can jeopardize both mind and body. Another of the speakers at the conference was South Africa's Nelson Mandela, who had been released earlier that year after serving more than twenty-five years of a life sentence for his struggle against apartheid. After his address, a small group of us met informally with Mandela, and someone asked him if he harbored any hatred for the people responsible for his life under apartheid and his decades in prison. "No!" he replied firmly. Hatred, he told us, robs people of the determination and energy needed to confront pressing issues. It consumes the one who holds it dear, he explained. The great leader won the Nobel Peace Prize himself in 1993, sharing it with F. W. de Klerk, who became president of South Africa after a life as a determined segregationist. It was de Klerk who released Mandela from prison and called for an end to the apartheid system.

Learning what Mandela had experienced and hearing him speak without rancor of those who had oppressed him, I thought deeply about my former patient and the enormous price she nearly paid for her destructive beliefs. Her intolerance had almost cost her her life. Dr. Brunschwig had given her both a rude awakening and a second chance to rid herself of two cancers: the first, prejudice, a malignancy of society; and the other a very real threat to her physical health. To her credit—and his—she apparently conquered both.

After completing their general surgery residencies, surgeons are eligible to apply for examination and certification by the American Board of Surgery. To be "board-certified" in one's specialty is an important distinction for all physicians with advanced training. I wanted to achieve board certification as soon as possible and took the two-part exam while I was still at Sloan-Kettering.

The first part, a written, multiple-choice test, was a broad-based review of surgery including diagnosis and treatment of numerous conditions. After passing the first part in New York in the fall of 1957, I was scheduled for the oral phase of the exam a few months later before a panel of distinguished surgeons assembled at Johns Hopkins University in Baltimore.

One of my board examiners was Dr. David Sabiston, then a junior faculty member at Hopkins and later the chief of surgery at Duke University. During the exam I'd answered several questions correctly and thought things were proceeding quite well when Dr. Sabiston, perhaps sensing my increasingly sanguine deportment, shot me a zinger.

"What is *dysphagia lusoria*?" he asked. I paused a moment, my mind a complete blank.

"Dysphagia lusoria," Dr. Sabiston repeated, "What is it?"

"I'm sorry, could you repeat the question?" I said, stalling for time. I was trying to put up a brave front, but my countenance undoubtedly betrayed my uncertainty. I vaguely recalled some kind of vascular anomaly syndrome associated with the esophagus, but couldn't discuss the details of the abnormality. Suddenly, it was too late. The examination was over.

As soon as I got home, I raced to my reference materials and anxiously looked up the accursed term that I feared had just derailed my promising career. Dysphagia lusoria, I read, is a condition in which the esophagus is compressed by a major blood vessel emerging from an abnormal location. If the board certified me, I prayed, I might even *specialize* in dysphagia lusoria!

Well, I did pass my boards, and years later had an opportunity to mention to Dr. Sabiston the distress his question had caused me.

"Oh, yes!" he recalled, his eyes twinkling. "When I asked you that question, you had already passed the examination! I was just probing deeper to check your fund of knowledge. As surgeons, you know, we have to maintain a delicate balance between confidence and humility. I merely wanted to shake you up a bit."

I took that lesson directly to heart. Later, when I became a board examiner myself, I made a point of asking two types of questions: confidence-building ones at the beginning of the exam and an ego-deflator or two closer toward the end if I thought the candidate was riding too high and needed to be brought down a peg—for his or her own good, of course.

As Sabiston said, surgeons have to maintain a delicate balance.

6

On to Munich:
Life as an Army Doctor

My treasured fellowship at Sloan-Kettering was due to end at the end of 1959, and it was time to honor my commitment to the Armed Forces. Leaving Ruthie in New York, I headed for Fort Sam Houston in San Antonio, Texas, to join about 500 physicians, dentists, and health care workers with similar obligations for a two-month orientation in military protocol, treatment of war casualties, and some rather rigorous physical training. Given that I've always been more of a bookworm than a jock, sprinting across an obstacle course weighted down with a loaded backpack took some getting used to. Pushups, panting through a long run, and swinging from rung to rung on a horizontal ladder weren't the sort of exercises I'd been brought up on, but the Army certainly whipped me into shape. Not before or since have I been in better physical condition.

The Armed Forces had been desegregated for more than a decade before I went on active duty, and I was surprisingly comfortable walking around on base, where—unlike in the civilian world—race generally didn't matter. But not all prejudice and preconceptions were expunged in a day, I soon learned.

I was one of only three blacks in my orientation class at Fort Sam, and soon after we arrived, my colleagues and I were assembled to complete a batch of military paperwork. The white sergeant in charge asked how many of us had specialty board certification, and I raised my hand along with a few white physicians. Looking directly at me, the sergeant barked, "I'm not talkin' about state board or national board certification, but *specialty* board certification!"

"Sergeant," I replied, "I *know* the difference." The others in the room roared with laughter at the condescending soldier being brought up short, and I took some satisfaction in standing my ground. I realized later, however, that my father would not have approved of my cockiness—no matter how right I was— and I regretted having embarrassed the sergeant in public.

"Never try to look good by making someone else look bad," my father would have said.

Off base, I was quickly reminded that things hadn't changed much in the South in more than a decade since I'd left to go to medical school in Washington, D.C. One evening, three fellow officers—all white—and I ventured into downtown San Antonio to go to the movies. The young woman in the ticket booth looked at me, looked at my white companions, looked back at me, and told *them* they could go into the theater but I couldn't. One of my colleagues looked at her in disbelief.

"Are you serious?" he asked. She was.

"Then we'll all leave," he said, and the four of us turned away.

I was stunned and angry. There I stood, a physician, a board-certified surgeon, a member of the Armed Forces serving my country, and I wasn't allowed the pleasure of watching a movie because of the color of my skin! My buddies were stung as well. It was a silent, painful ride back to base for us all.

Most of us doctors weren't military people by nature, and the Army really had no illusions about turning us into professional soldiers, but we were expected to learn the basics and observe military protocol. For instance, we came into service as captains and were required to salute any superior officer we encountered, meaning majors and above. We could tell who those above us were because anyone higher than a captain wore a cap with gold braid known as "scrambled eggs" on the visor. Most of us figured out how to recognize the so-called field-grade officers in time to snap a crisp salute: right elbow cocked, fingers extended, tips just brushing the visor of the cap. I must say we did have a couple of people in our unit who could have been court-martialed for their inability to get even that basic motion down.

After orientation, I had orders to report to the Army's Second Field Hospital in Munich, Germany. Although Ruthie and I were looking forward to living in Europe, I was initially disappointed to learn we were going to Munich, a place I had long associated with one of history's monumental misjudgments. I recalled what British Prime Minister Neville Chamberlain had said after signing the Munich Agreement with Adolf Hitler and Benito Mussolini on September 29, 1938, that the pact to appease Hitler represented "peace for our time." That was only months before Hitler launched World War II.

After we got there, I found Munich one of the most interesting, enjoyable, and mind-broadening places I'd ever been. The citizens of Munich are known for their *gemütlichkeit*, or good-natured disposition and congeniality, and Ruthie and I chose to live in the city rather than on the base in order to learn the language faster and make friends with the German people. A German surgical colleague at the Army hospital, Dr. Andreas Schnur, helped us find a cozy new apartment. Ruthie got a job at Radio Free Europe, thanks to the assistance of Dr. Guy Robbins, a Sloan-Kettering mentor of mine who knew the American director, and we quickly began absorbing the customs and culture of southern Germany.

We had been in Munich only a few months when my old FAMC chums, Julian "Cannonball" Adderley and his brother Nat, arrived to give a jazz concert as part of a multi-city European tour. Ruthie and I got front-row center seats, and we had a fabulous reunion with the musicians, who by that time had attained world renown.

The two of us had a pact: to visit all the historic and cultural sites we could whenever we traveled. Munich opened up a whole wide world of Old Masters, the Alte Pinakotek, the Deutsche Museum, the idyllic Englischer Garten (where Radio Free Europe's offices were located) and, of course, the famous Oktoberfest, where we sang, danced, and drank beer with the best of them. I gave my mother a birthday trip to Munich, and she also visited many of the city's historic sites.

My tour in Munich occurred during the Cold War when Berlin was divided and therefore off limits for military personnel to visit, so we didn't get to see East Germany while I was in the service. Ruthie and I have visited Berlin twice since the Wall came down and reunification took place, making our tour of Germany complete.

Being from Florida where snow was practically unheard of, I had always dreamed of learning to ski, and Munich was close to the famous ski resorts at Berchtesgaden and Garmisch-Partenkirchen. Maybe I wasn't a jock, but I had often fantasized about deftly schussing down slopes of pristine powder, craggy alps above and picturesque villages in the valleys below. On my very first night on duty in the emergency room at the hospital, however, an Army flight surgeon who had hitched a military flight from Goose Bay, Labrador, to go skiing in Garmisch was brought in with a severe knee injury from a fall his first day on the slopes. He had torn the ligaments in the joint and required major surgery. (That was before arthroscopic techniques were developed to make knee surgery an in-and-out procedure.) The orthopedic surgeons on staff fixed him up, but I decided not to take a chance on winding up in the OR myself. So much for my dreams of becoming a downhill skier!

With my desire to study foreign languages, I took full advantage of my two-year tour of duty in Munich to study German. The University of Maryland had a Munich branch that I attended for three hours in the evening twice weekly for twelve weeks. When we began there were twenty-three of us, all Americans determined to study and learn German. By the end of the first month there were eleven, and only six of us completed the course. I did manage to get fairly good, if not fluent, in German, and I'm convinced my language study was more valuable than skiing would have been.

Drs. Schnur and Peter Schroeder helped me with conversational German and introduced me to the writings of the country's literary giants. I studied diligently, and before we came home, I had learned enough to read Goethe and Friedrich Schiller in their original forms. I never pretended to be fluent, but I could communicate and comprehend reasonably well.

Colonel Arthur Cohen, a regular Army officer and specialist in vascular surgery, was chief of the hospital's surgical department, and he named me chief of general surgery, a section that had a complement of five surgeons. In that position, I made daily rounds with my team, saw patients in the surgical clinic, and performed routine operations such as removing benign tumors, repairing hernias, and occasionally performing a mastectomy or an intestinal resection for patients diagnosed with cancer. We took out gallbladders quite often and removed varicose veins, a procedure rarely performed today because normal veins were taken out with the varicosities, which are now used in coronary artery surgery as replacements.

The patients in an Army field hospital in peacetime are generally young and don't typically require the complex operations I had learned to perform at Sloan-Kettering, but I was kept plenty busy. We held weekly teaching sessions to discuss our complications and deaths (fortunately, these were rare). We also held conferences to discuss various surgical topics. These academic sessions were stimulating and informative, as I recall.

One regular nuisance, however, was the disaster drill. I *was* in the Army, after all, and doctors weren't immune from the need for constant readiness. We were thus always on call. Mock attacks on the base were part of life, and physicians had to become accustomed to being jarred awake at odd hours of the night and ordered to report to duty immediately. I learned to live with it, and life in Munich was getting so comfortable I started to feel a little apprehensive about returning home.

My routine was shattered when the German-born widow of an American soldier came to the hospital with a diagnosis of gallstones and intermittent jaundice. I proposed removing her gallbladder and doing exploratory bile duct surgery to find the cause of the problem. After consulting with several of my German civilian and military colleagues, she agreed to the operation, and the surgery went without a hitch.

The patient was recuperating well, and I expected her to make a full recovery when, three days later, she developed postoperative pancreatitis with severe abdominal pain, abdominal distension, nausea, and vomiting. My team and I inserted a tube into her stomach to remove secretions and decrease stimulation of the pancreas. We administered antibiotics and analgesics to her and gave her fluids and electrolytes, but her condition continued to deteriorate. Within a few days, she was dead.

I was devastated. She was the only patient I lost during my military experience, and haunting, disturbing questions nagged me for days, weeks, and months afterward. Was it my fault? Could I have prevented it? Should I have foreseen it? Even years later, the answers are elusive.

It is well known that pancreatitis can develop after operations on the biliary tract, possibly due to surgical manipulation, a chemical irritation from the bile, or the use of some medications. While there is no way to know exactly what happened in this case, all I knew was that this woman had come in for elective surgery, had entrusted herself to my care, and she was dead.

After the funeral, her family asked to see me. I invited her grown children to my office, not knowing what they would say to me. One of the woman's daughters spoke first. In a mixture of German and English, her voice soft and timid, choked with emotion, she said: "Dr. Leffall, we know you're busy, and we don't want to keep you away from your duties. But we want to tell you and your colleagues that we know you did all you could to save our mother, and we are very grateful."

I was relieved, of course, that they had come to express appreciation and not anger, and I thanked her for the kind words. The daughter then handed me a small package that she said her mother had planned to give me on her first postoperative visit. She asked me to open it before they left. In the box was a small wooden bowl with the inscription: "To Captain LaSalle D. Leffall, Jr.—In grateful appreciation."

Turning the bowl over and over in my hands, struck by both its beauty and its meaning, I struggled to maintain my composure. I had gone over and over the details of the surgery and of its fatal complications, but could come up with no stisfactory answer to explain the tragedy that resulted. Yet there I was, thanking the patient's family for their confidence in me. I told them that I was grateful their mother had thought enough of me to allow me to do the operation. We did everything we knew to do, I said, and I expressed my personal remorse that as the surgeon, the captain of the team, I had been unable to save her. I almost lost my composure at that point, but I hung on while they filed out, as quietly and humbly as they had come. Trembling, I locked the door to my office for the solitude I so sorely needed.

I received some solace from the absolution granted me by the bereaved family, but I have never gotten over the feeling of sudden, unexpected defeat and especially the loss of a patient's life.

Physicians—like families—have to learn to muster their strength and find the courage to move ahead, no matter what happens. Their memories, of course, are different from those of their patients and their patients' families, but they don't forget.

7

I Begin Where I Began:
Returning to Howard and the Ideal Job

Throughout my schooling, I had always planned to return to Tallahassee to practice surgery and live somewhere near the Famcee campus where I had so enjoyed my undergraduate life. I figured Quincy was too small to support a black surgeon, but I could easily imagine a professional life in Tallahassee with the added joys of campus culture. Many meetings of black medical groups were held at Famcee, and I foresaw a happy, challenging time growing old back home in Florida. That was before I went to Sloan-Kettering.

Midway through my first year in New York City, I started to grasp the idea that my training in cancer surgery would be better applied in a large metropolitan area. I was, after all, only the third black who had attained the benefit of the experience I was getting at Memorial Sloan-Kettering, and although I was sure I could make a perfectly good living in Florida, I realized I would probably be the only doctor in that part of the state—black or white—with my level of specialization. At that time, most hospitals in that state still were not open to blacks, which further limited my opportunities.

I was also thinking more and more about my desire to teach. I remembered how much fun I'd had teaching anatomy at Howard Med before the "cadaver walk," and I had enjoyed my teaching responsibilities as chief surgical resident there the year before, helping medical students and less senior residents learn the ropes.

Even more fundamental to my plans was the sense of obligation that had been instilled in me by my father to use my skills to assist others. One shouldn't just earn a living, he said, one should, in the familiar usage of today, "give back" to the people and institutions that need our help. With that in mind, my focus increasingly turned to teaching at Howard.

It was the dawn of the civil rights era. The Supreme Court had ruled three years earlier that "separate-but-equal" schools were inherently unequal and unconstitutional; and one year before, the black citizens of Montgomery, Alabama, had won their boycott demanding the right to sit anywhere on a public bus. But great barriers fall slowly, and there weren't yet many opportunities for black physicians outside predominantly black hospitals.

I was still living in a "black" world. There were very few places from which to choose for professional practice. Homer Phillips and Harlem hospitals had residents, but those institutions weren't affiliated with medical schools, which meant that if I wanted to teach medical students I would have to go either to Howard or to Meharry in Nashville. Drs. Syphax and Jack White, the two professors who had taught me the most about surgery, were at Howard, which made that an exciting prospect. Perhaps even more important was that I was very conscious even then—as I am today—that if it hadn't been for Howard University College of Medicine agreeing to take me in that summer of 1948, there is a very real possibility I would never have been able to fulfill my childhood dream of becoming a doctor. I owed my allegiance to Howard and was thrilled at the thought of returning.

While I was still in New York I talked about my future with Syphax, who by that time was head of the Department of Surgery at Howard Med, and with White, who was head of the cancer program that would later become the Howard University Cancer Center. They both knew I still had the Army ahead of me, but they invited me to join their practice when I completed my military obligation. That meant I would be performing surgery at Freedmen's and still be able to teach at the medical school. It was my dream job!

While I was thinking about it, however, a close friend and colleague told me I shouldn't return to Howard because I would not be able to accomplish anything of substance there. I would find no real support from the administration, my friend claimed, and colleagues elsewhere would not include me in national programs and committees because I would be based at a black medical school and would not be taken seriously by the medical establishment. He didn't know it, but his reasoning simply hardened my resolve to return to my medical alma mater. I was *determined* to prove him wrong. It is also true that at that time my options, as a black doctor, were limited. It is highly unlikely that I would have obtained a faculty position at a white medical school. However, I thought little about that possibility because of my allegiance to Howard and my desire to return there.

Ruthie thought going back to Howard would be wonderful. We would be in Washington, D.C., again, which both of us loved, and she would be only a couple hours' drive from her family's home in Richmond.

Knowing I would be going back to the states to teach made me eager to learn all I could about the practice of surgery in Europe. Before World War II it was common for American academic surgeons to gain some experience in Europe, and although the United States vaulted to one of the top nations in the medical world after the war, there was still tremendous respect for the leading surgical institutions of Europe, particularly those in Germany and Austria. I made a point of trying to visit as many as possible while overseas.

The most-coveted surgical post in Germany at that time was held by Professor Rudolf Zenker, chief of surgery at Munich Hospital. Berlin had been considered the top place to be before the war, but it was then surrounded by Communist-ruled East Germany, and Munich became the surgeon's Mecca. Dr. Zenker invited three of us from the American military hospital to be his guests for a day, and I was among the trio chosen to have an opportunity to watch him operate. Of course, I accepted immediately.

Zenker was slated to perform a procedure exploring the common bile duct. As we American doctors observed from inside the OR, he inserted a probe into the duct and was trying to see if the shiny metal tool had entered the duodenum, the first part of the small intestine. He then began looking for a clear indication that the metal of the probe was visible through the barely translucent wall of the duodenum, seeking what we surgeons call a "steel sign" through the tissue. As Zenker probed the patient's bile duct, I asked in German if I could ask him a question. In the operating room of an American teaching hospital, there would be nothing unusual about that, but I could feel Zenker's minions staring at me from around the table as I broke the protocol of silence. I asked anyway, "I don't see the steel sign, Professor Zenker. Can you tell us that you're in the duodenum and not pushing one wall against another?"

"I can't prove to you that I'm in the duodenum," the great surgeon replied calmly, "but I *know* I am." The professor had spoken, and whether I could see it or not, that meant the steel had reached the duodenum.

"Schluss," came the muffled comment of a German colleague next to me. I knew what *that* meant all right. The conversation was over.

Toward the end of our visit, the three of us returned to

Zenker's office for refreshments and relaxed conversation. There he spoke about the close relationship that existed between German and American surgical colleagues both before and after World War II, and there was no evidence of any hard feelings that I had spoken out of turn.

Whenever I traveled in those early days I tried to visit the leading surgical centers in the cities where I stayed. One of the most memorable was the office of Professor Theodor Billroth, the famed chief of surgery at the University of Vienna who performed the first successful partial removal of the stomach to excise a cancerous lesion in 1881. The head of the department was away, but he had arranged for one of his associates to show me around. Dr. Billroth's desk, some of the instruments he used for the operation, and an article describing his techniques were on display. As one interested in the field, I could feel the presence of history as I examined them. Billroth, a lover of classical music and a close friend of the composer Johannes Brahms, is still recognized as the leading gastrointestinal-tract surgeon of all time and as a pathfinder who opened new vistas for those seeking cures for intractable diseases. I am proud to call myself a member of his profession.

My tour of duty in Germany was thus enlightening and enjoyable, both professionally and personally. Ruthie and I visited most of the countries in Europe, becoming more familiar with their customs and culture. Having the opportunity to head my team at the Second Field Hospital taught me more about leadership and the importance of teamwork and fair play. Further, I was continuing to hone my technical and diagnostic surgical skills.

My obligation to the military was up in December 1961, and I happily returned to civilian life. Ruthie and I went directly back to the nation's capital and rented a friend's apartment in the upper Northwest section of the city while we looked for a place of our own, which we found in Southwest Washington, a long-neglected area that was then part of an ambitious urban renewal project. It was the early days of the Kennedy administration, and lots of bright young people were moving to Southwest, where they could afford to live in town, close to their government offices, and be around others who were flocking to the city to join in the excitement of being among JFK's "new generation of Americans."

We found a new townhouse at 1300 Fourth Street SW and quickly made friends with our neighbors. One of them was Clifford Alexander, a young lawyer who had just joined the administration as a foreign affairs officer on the National Security Council staff. We've been close friends ever since. He was the first black secretary of the Army in the Carter administration and recently served as chairman and CEO of Dun and Bradstreet. Another neighbor was Roger Wilkins, who was then special assistant to the administrator of the Agency for International Development at the State Department. Roger has had a distinguished career in government and academia and is currently the Clarence J. Robinson Professor of History and American Culture at George Mason University.

We also became friends with the journalist Carl Rowan, who lived in the city but not in Southwest. Carl was one of the first black commissioned officers in the Navy and had distinguished himself as a writer for the *Minneapolis Tribune* before joining the Kennedy administration. He later was named ambassador to Finland and director of the U.S. Information Agency. After he left government, Carl wrote a nationally syndicated column and numerous books. He became a familiar face to millions of Americans as a regular commentator on Washington talk shows. He was also the first black president of a peculiar Washington institution called the Gridiron Club.

Gridiron Club membership is limited to a few dozen print journalists who annually throw a white-tie dinner at which they stage a musical roast of their sources, including their guest of honor, who is always the president of the United States. On several occasions, Carl invited me to be his guest at these dinners, including the year he served as president of the Club when, by tradition, he had to give his speech in utter darkness.

Another friend from those days was Earl Graves, a New Yorker who was then working on Bobby Kennedy's staff. Earl went into business after the senator was killed in 1968 and later founded *Black Enterprise* magazine. He has always paid special attention to medical subjects and devoted whole issues to the best black specialists in various areas. I was honored to be on the cover of his wonderful magazine twice.

Ruthie and I both decided that she wouldn't go back to work right away upon our return to Washington, and by spring she had good reason: she was pregnant. We didn't really plan it that way, but we were thrilled. Our son Donney—formally LaSalle Doheny Leffall III—was born on Sunday morning, January 6, 1963, almost exactly one year after our return to the states.

I was attending a surgical meeting the night Ruthie went into labor, and her good friend Joanne Ewing, then a third-year medical student rotating on the OB/GYN service, drove her to Freedmen's Hospital. I got to the hospital shortly after she was admitted. Dr. Harry Martin, a Howard graduate and an excellent physician, delivered Donney without complication.

I was present in the obstetrical suite but not in the delivery room. That was a few years before it became common practice to let fathers witness the birth of their children. Dr. Martin brought my son out to me a few minutes later. The baby boy was crying lustily. He reminded me of what my mother's obstetrician, Dr. Foote, had said about me when I was born: that I made so much noise on arrival he imagined I'd make a good singer or public speaker.

Donney's birth triggered powerful feelings of tenderness, protectiveness, fear, and love within me, emotions I knew but had never felt in quite the same way before. Holding him in my arms for the first time, just minutes after his birth, I thought: If I can be a fraction of the father to him that my father was to me, he'll grow up just fine.

As Ruthie and I gazed at the tiny, wrinkled newborn when I joined her in her hospital room, we tried to figure out whom he resembled more. Ruthie, of course, insisted that he resembled her while I proclaimed proudly and confidently that he looked more like me. In my heart, I think she was right, but we both agreed he was the most beautiful baby we'd ever seen.

Like any parent, I have enduring memories of Donney growing up. One is of him walking around with his Batman cape and hood at about three-years-old. On another occasion, he knocked over a lamp in the living room and broke it. When his mother saw the damage, Donney immediately tried to shift the blame elsewhere. "Daddy broke the lamp," he insisted. "Daddy broke it." It was one of the few times I ever spanked him.

When he was about seven-and-a-half-years-old, Donney started playing tennis, so we purchased a special racket for him that had a regular head and strings but a handle adjusted for his size. He went to tennis camp and quickly excelled at the game. He could beat me by the time he was eleven. Of course, I've never laid any claim to being an athlete, but I am an avid tennis player, and playing with Donney became one of our favorite father–son activities. He went on to play for the varsity tennis team at St. Albans, the Episcopal school for boys he attended in Washington, and later for Harvard's freshman team.

I admit I tried more than once to persuade Donney to follow my footsteps into medicine, but the sciences just weren't his thing. His passion lay in the liberal arts, particularly history and economics, and I'm tremendously proud of the course he chose. When Donney took an interest in business and law, he was fortunate to have as a mentor his godfather and our longtime friend Wesley Williams, a prominent lawyer and past chairman of the Federal Reserve Board of Richmond.

It is no surprise, however, given my own upbringing, that I

stressed to Donney the importance of a strong education. Ruthie and I have always reminded our son that he was blessed with both ability and opportunity and that he should use them to make a difference in the world around him. He has never disappointed us. Like his mother, Donney has an infectious sense of humor combined with a genuine intellectual curiosity. He has made us both so proud.

Donney earned his bachelor's degree magna cum laude, his law degree cum laude, and a business degree with second-year honors, all from Harvard. He became a lawyer and then an investment banker, but after the terrorist attacks on September 11, 2001, he decided to spend at least a few years serving in the nonprofit sector. As I write this, he is president and chief operating officer of the National Housing Partnership Foundation, which helps to provide affordable apartments for low- and moderate-income families.

Ruthie deserves a lot of the credit for rearing such a wonderful son. While I was a young faculty member climbing the academic ladder, trying to make my presence known, it was she who drove Donney to his soccer games, who carpooled him and his classmates, served on school committees, and generally fulfilled the role of a great mom.

I was thirty-one years old when I joined the surgical faculty at Howard as assistant professor, with the primary responsibilities of teaching third- and fourth-year medical students, training surgical residents, and engaging in clinical research that could lead to publications. I was fortunate to join my two mentors, Drs. Syphax and White, as a junior partner in their surgical practice. This association not only broadened my contacts in the patient community but also allowed me to learn from two highly respected surgeons.

I was busy learning the new practice, but I didn't have many patients yet, so whenever there was a conference on surgery or cancer that I could attend, I went in order to stay abreast of new concepts and techniques and to make further contacts in my field. At Sloan-Kettering I had been advised to join the American Cancer Society, so when I settled in Washington I became a member of the society's District of Columbia division.

To get established, I studied the records of surgical patients at Freedmen's Hospital and wrote papers for medical journals, coauthoring them with my better-known senior colleagues. White and I produced many papers on cancer; Syphax and I wrote on general surgery. Our articles didn't make for popular reading, but we three frequently reported findings of complex research on topics such as "Clinical Aids in Strangulation Obstruction," which described how to diagnose an emergency condition in which a person's blood supply to the small intestine is cut off. We also authored several papers on cancer of the colon and rectum as well as cancer of the breast.

It was the mid-1960s, and American physicians were just beginning to focus on statistics showing that a disproportionate number of African-Americans were dying of cancer. Our work illuminating this disparity was published in numerous peer-review journals such as the *American Journal of Surgery*, the *Archives of Surgery*, the *Annals of Surgery,* and *Cancer.*

In the spring of 1973 an article appeared in the journal *Cancer* entitled, "Alarming Increase of the Cancer Mortality in the U.S. Black Population (1950–1967)." The study reported on by that article, led by Ulrich K. Henschke, who held both M.D. and Ph.D. degrees, disclosed that deaths from cancer were not only growing among blacks in the United States, but were increasing *twice* as fast as cancer deaths among whites. No one knew why, although some speculated that environmental factors had a lot to do with it. Henschke, whom White and I had recruited from Sloan-Kettering to come to Howard as chief of radiation oncology, was listed first among the article's six authors. My name was second. Jack White and three less senior researchers were named as well including a young surgical oncologist, Roy Schneider. Our study didn't break new ground in the sense that it made no attempt to propose a new treatment for cancer or explore previously unknown causes of the disease. It simply looked at numbers that had been around for years and pointed out a truly shocking trend that had escaped the notice of nearly all researchers up to that time.

We Howard doctors knew from our own experience practicing in a predominantly black hospital that the cure rate for black cancer patients was poorer than that for whites, and we sensed the situation was getting worse. Our analysis of the numbers proved us right. That article, preliminary as it was, focused attention on the special vulnerability of blacks to cancer. I like to think that it led not only to more and better studies but also to a better understanding of how to deal with a serious national health crisis.

I was also trying to get as much operating-room experience as I could during these early years. I took call more often than did my senior colleagues, meaning I was the person summoned in an emergency or when a surgeon was needed and the patient didn't have one. I also operated with Freedmen's residents three or four days a week on hospital cases. Typically, if someone was diagnosed with a disorder that might require surgery, a resident would be assigned to the case, but residents always had to have an attending physician with them when they operated. I would often play that role. In those cases, the resident would wield the knife, but the attending physician would be there to give advice or take over if something unexpected occurred.

That was one way I fulfilled my role as a teacher. There are basically three methods doctors use to teach medicine, however. The classroom lecture is one, but unlike other disciplines, it is probably the least interesting and effective in my field. Coursework is certainly necessary to build up one's core knowledge of medicine and surgery, but it is no substitute for on-the-job training. Medical students learn more by presenting cases to their professors, discussing the disease process, abnormal physiology along with the appropriate diagnostic and treatment measures. The third method is by working in the clinical environment with real patients in the clinic, ward, operating room, and emergency department.

When students make rounds with an Attending in the morning, they see all sorts of cases and every kind of patient. It's a great opportunity to explain to them the subtleties they need to know to differentiate between various possibilities and to show them techniques for questioning and examining patients. As the attending physician, third-year students would have to present their cases to me. Each student was assigned a patient and had to know the basic science and surgical aspects of that patient's case before presenting me with all the details.

I have always enjoyed such presentations the most, and I often tell my students that they can't just try to "wing it" when they have to make presentations. They must each learn to present a case properly, working from notes but not reading. They must also be able to explain why a patient may have appendicitis and not cholecystitis (inflammation of the gallbladder), why they're looking at an ulcer and not pancreatitis, or what makes something a case of GERD (gastro-esophageal reflux disease) and not cancer of the esophagus. Lectures just aren't interactive enough for that.

The same is true of making rounds. Walking through a hospital ward, students can actually take a dressing off and look at a wound and see it firsthand. No two-dimensional photograph in a book, regardless of its quality and technical merit, can teach a future physician as much.

I also served for thirty years as a surgical consultant at Walter Reed Army Medical Center in Washington, where I taught not only that hospital's surgical residents but also students from the military medical school, the Uniformed Services University of the Health Sciences in Bethesda, Maryland. Some of the most challenging surgical cases from U.S. armed forces around the world are brought to Walter Reed for treatment, which gives both residents and students the opportunity to see cases they would rarely encounter in another hospital.

Then and now I always tell my students that at the end of each day they should ask themselves two questions about their medical practice: "What did I do today that I shouldn't have done?" and "What didn't I do that I should have done?" Only when these questions are answered honestly and asked repeatedly over the course of their lives can physicians gain the ability to improve human lives.

To me, the role of the teacher is to instruct, to inspire, to stimulate, to impart ethical and moral values, to stretch the imagination, and to expand the aspirations of others. When I became a faculty member at Howard, I tried to take the excellent teaching points I had learned from my own teachers and shape them into what would become the "Leffall method." Drs. Cobb, Drew, Syphax, and White served as superb role models.

I love teaching.

Three years after I joined the faculty at Howard, President James Nabrit asked me to become dean of the medical school. It was a heady honor for a thirty-five-year-old junior faculty member, but I had to turn him down. I had spent most of my life studying to be a surgeon and a cancer specialist, and I believed the deanship would take me away from the profession I loved. It would also keep me away from teaching, although as dean I would still have had some interaction with medical students, particularly when there was a problem.

Five years later, I did fill in as acting dean for a few months, and I got a taste of the thankless job I had refused. Few people, I discovered, go out of their way to praise a dean. It demands a knack for troubleshooting, mediating disputes, and the patience of Job. But having done it for only a few months, I formed a special relationship with the class of 1970 and got to sign the students' M.D. degrees that year. Three decades later, the president of that class, Dr. Alvin Bryant, said in presenting my portrait to the college for hanging on the "Wall of Deans" that I had inspired him to become a surgeon. Honored as I am to have my picture up there with the others, I've always felt I escaped with only a fraction of the headaches my colleagues on that wall endured.

When I completed my acting deanship, I was named chair of the Department of Surgery succeeding Mickey Syphax, who voluntarily stepped aside in order for me to assume this position. I will be forever grateful to him for that magnanimous gesture. Dr. James Hardy of the University of Mississippi, a leading surgical academician, later pulled me aside at a medical meeting to tell me, "LaSalle, now that you've become the professor and chief, I have two bits of advice for you: Never stop operating, because that is the one thing that separates you from your nonsurgical teaching colleagues, and never, *ever* stop teaching students!" I've diligently followed his advice throughout my career.

To head Howard's Department of Surgery for twenty-five years, from 1970 to 1995, was a special privilege and honor. In addition to continuing the department's emphasis on excellent patient care, I wanted to focus on the following areas: 1) student teaching, 2) resident training, 3) research opportunities, 4) faculty recruitment, and 5) active involvement in various surgical organizations.

Working closely with my mentor and predecessor Mickey Syphax and my vice chair Clive Callender, who succeeded me as chair in 1996, I stressed training residents to become safe, competent surgeons and teaching surgical principles to medical students. I took pride in my faculty's efforts to stimulate students to pursue surgical careers. Recruitment of talented faculty remained a high priority under my chairmanship. When I assumed the post there were twelve divisions in the department—anesthesiology, cardiovascular surgery, thoracic surgery, general surgery, neurosurgery, ophthalmologic surgery, orthopedic surgery, otolaryngology/head and neck surgery, plastic and reconstructive surgery, surgical oncology, transplant surgery, and urological surgery. Two divisions were subsequently granted departmental status—anesthesiology in 1989 and ophthalmology in 2000.

When I became department chair I also initiated the annual Drew/Syphax Lecture and Seminar to pay tribute to Drs. Charles Drew and Burke Syphax. That event brings together leading surgical academicians, who are invited to share their experiences with us and present our students and residents with different perspectives. The first lecturer was Dr. Walter Ballinger and the most recent, in 2005—the thirty-fifth—was Dr. Julie Ann Freischlag, the first female chief of surgery at Johns Hopkins University Hospital. Dr. Claude Organ has given the lecture twice, in 1986 when we celebrated the fiftieth anniversary of our residency program, and again in 2004 when he was president of the American College of Surgeons. Organ has also been chairman of the American Board of Surgery and is co-author of the textbook, *A Century of Black Surgeons: The USA Experience.*

Howard's general surgical residency, begun in 1936, has always been fully approved by the Residency Review Committee, the national organization that certifies medical training programs. As director of the residency program during my chairmanship, I remain proud to state that this record reflects the broad training that our residents historically receive, combined with their passing rates on the American Board of Surgery examination. Reflecting the increased numbers of women in medical school, Howard's general surgery residency is currently approximately 60 percent female. Five residents per year complete the program.

The contributions of the Howard surgical faculty have been critical in helping the department achieve its goals in student and resident education and performance. Most of the general surgery residents spend two years in research at some of our nation's major research centers after their second or third year of postgraduate training. The residency consists of five clinical years; the research years are extra. During my tenure as chairman my staff and I made attempts to establish a full-time research laboratory but were unsuccessful because of university financial and personnel constraints. Research experience for our residents remains a high priority, however.

As chair I encouraged all surgical faculty members to be active participants in their national and international specialty societies. For me this meant involvement with the American Cancer Society, the Society of Surgical Oncology, and the American College of Surgeons. These relationships, I believe, helped us all promote departmental goals related to the exchange of information on surgical education and research.

One measure of a successful medical program is the caliber of the people from other schools who agree to make guest appearances and participate in your program's activities. In 1986, for example, I invited Dr. Dean Warren of the Emory University School of Medicine to Howard. Dr. Warren was at the time president-elect of the American College of Surgeons, and I asked him to come for a reception marking the fiftieth anniversary of the department's residency program. Congressman Augustus Hawkins of California assisted us in getting a room in the Rayburn House Office Building on Capitol Hill for this special occasion. That night Dean was in his usual gregarious mood. He chatted candidly and enthusiastically with several of our medical students, residents, and faculty, and he helped make the evening a great success. Then he returned to Atlanta and a few days later underwent major surgery to remove his left eye and upper jaw in a desperate and ultimately unsuccessful attempt to halt the spread of a radiation-resistant carcinoma of the maxillary sinus. Not once during his visit did he give even the slightest clue of what he was facing, nor did he ever mention, when I saw him and thanked him afterward, what a tremendous favor he had done us by coming to our celebration knowing about his life-threatening illness and imminent surgery.

Since then I have tried to remember Dean Warren's remarkable personal courage and commitment to his profession and friends. When someone asks me to do something, I either agree readily or—when I must—I offer my regrets, thinking of Warren's example. When I agree, however, I try not to make the person who extended the invitation feel guilty by reciting any sacrifices I may have made in order to accept it.

Perhaps all of us would like a taste of immortality, or at least the knowledge that our names will live after us, both in our children and in our work. I am proud to hold the Charles R. Drew chair in surgery at Howard today because it reminds anyone who cares that the famed blood researcher is part of Howard Med's very soul. It also shows me that my colleagues thought highly enough of me to honor me with a named professorship.

When Dr. Charles H. Epps was dean of the College of Medicine, he pointed out that Howard had only one such endowed chair at the time but that it should have had more in order to attract and retain top faculty. After he had successfully raised the money for the Drew chair, he came to me and asked me for a list of names of people we could contact to find the $1.5 million we would need to name a professorship in my honor. I was humbled. Thanks to our generous friends and colleagues, the process of raising the money took only eighteen months. Today Dr. Clive O. Callender, a leader in minority organ transplantation and my successor as chair of the Department of Surgery, is the LaSalle D. Leffall, Jr., professor of surgery.

Epps raised money for three more endowed chairs during his eight-year tenure. In each case, 10 percent of the earnings from the endowment goes toward increasing the size of the fund itself. The rest is spent on special research, education, or a salary stipend in consultation with the holder of the chair.

One by-product of a successful career in academic medicine is being invited to give visiting lectures at medical schools and professional societies around the world. Not long after I accepted the chairmanship of Howard's Department of Surgery in 1970, I was asked to return to St. Louis to speak at Homer

Phillips Hospital, where I had done my internship. It was one of my first such appearances, and I spent hours researching and refining my text on early diagnosis and treatment of colorectal cancer. When I walked into the lecture hall, I was crestfallen to see that only a dozen physicians had shown up for my homecoming. A few more came in later, but I confess I was disappointed at the turnout. I tried to conceal that, however, and delivered my presentation as enthusiastically and eloquently as if I were speaking to a full house.

Afterward, a tall, affable surgeon came up to the lectern to say he'd been impressed by my lecture and would like me to become involved in academic surgical committee work. He mentioned the American Surgical Association's Study of Surgical Services in the United States, a landmark research project known throughout our profession as the SOSSUS study. I was thrilled to be considered for such an important project, but I had no idea who the man was. He was Dr. Walter F. Ballinger, chief of surgery at Washington University, one of the country's most distinguished surgeons. That lecture turned out to be a major breakthrough for me. Ballinger opened doors, not only to the SOSSUS but also to a lifetime in the world of academic surgery on a national scale. But it would never have happened if I had let my displeasure show in my lecture and not given a first-rate presentation.

The next year I was asked to return to my home state to make an appearance at the University of Florida School of Medicine. I had no idea what I was in for when I accepted the invitation. Visiting professors usually give a lecture, make rounds at the hospital, and review a couple of particularly challenging cases with the residents. When I received the itinerary for my trip to Gainesville, however, I was surprised to discover that I was actually expected to perform an operation there. It's not that I minded performing surgery, of course, but the added duty seemed quite out of the ordinary.

Dr. Edward Woodward, chair of the department of surgery,

who had issued the invitation, explained that his students insisted I be the primary surgeon in the OR during my visit. No black surgeon had ever operated at the university's hospital, and they wanted me to be the first.

When I arrived on campus, Dr. Patrick O'Leary, a young assistant professor who later became chief of surgery at Louisiana State University, informed me that I was to operate the next day on a patient with an intractable gastric ulcer. Not knowing what to expect, I envisioned an obese patient who'd undergone a previous abdominal operation that left numerous postoperative intra-abdominal adhesions (fibrous tissue that may cause obstruction of the small intestine). I expected plenty of complications.

That evening, after being granted temporary surgical privileges, I visited the patient in the hospital and found a thin, sixty-year-old white male with no history of previous abdominal operations. I explained to him that I would be his surgeon. Having already been informed of this by the university surgical staff, he readily agreed.

I returned to the hospital the next morning to perform the surgery. Assisted by several surgical residents, I removed the lower half of the patient's stomach and joined it to the duodenum, the first part of the small intestine. We completed the operation "skin-to-skin" in less than an hour, and the patient made a smooth recovery. He was back to normal in a few weeks. I had broken another barrier.

At about that time, Dr. R. Lee Clark, the first president of M. D. Anderson Cancer Center, and Dr. Jonathan Rhoads, chief of surgery at the University of Pennsylvania, two powerful forces in oncology, recommended me for membership on the American College of Surgeons' Commission on Cancer, where I met many of the nation's leaders in oncology. I began from then on to develop a new, valuable, and very influential group of colleagues in my chosen profession at a level higher than I had ever imagined.

8

Wielding the Knife:
Humility and Responsibility
in Surgical Practice

Early in my career a woman came into my office with a tentative diagnosis of a tumor in her large intestine. An X-ray done during a barium enema showed a lesion, but the radiologist couldn't decide whether it was cancerous. That was before colonoscopy was introduced in the early 1970s, and the only way a physician could determine the nature of the growth was to operate.

I informed the patient that there was a good possibility we were looking at a malignant tumor and that it would have to be removed. I further explained that if the tumor was attached to any other of her organs we would also have to remove all or part of those organs to prevent further spread of the disease. I assured her we would leave her body as normal as possible and not do anything that wasn't required, but I asked for her permission in advance to do what was necessary once we surgeons could see what we were dealing with.

I always try to talk to patients face to face in a situation like that—never on the phone—and with another close family member present if they want one. Sometimes patients want to hear it for themselves first and don't want anyone else there. I prefer telling them what they're facing with as much sensitivity and compassion and caring as I can. I speak in an unhurried manner, use a modulated tone, and try not to be an alarmist. Then I tell the patient the truth.

I always try to offer hope—because I truly believe no case is ever hopeless—but I do tell the truth. I learned that lesson the hard way.

Once, as a young physician, I had a patient who had cancer of the breast. Her husband said, "Don't tell her; she can't take it."

"How can I not?" I asked.

"Tell her it wasn't cancer but it would have turned into cancer if you hadn't removed her breast," he advised.

That path was against my better judgment, but I went along with the husband, and shortly after the patient got out of the hospital, she asked to come see me.

Once in my office, she rushed over to me and shook her finger in my face. "Dr. Leffall," she said, " you *lied* to me!" I didn't know what to say.

"Who deserved to know more than *I* do?" she demanded. "My husband's not the patient. *I'm* the patient! *I'm* the *patient!*"

I suddenly felt like a complete neophyte. I was wrong. From that day to this one, I always tell my patients the truth.

I followed that rule before I operated on the patient I mentioned above with the intestinal lesion because after we had performed the surgery, she knew the news could be either okay or pretty grim.

Following my usual procedure, I visited the patient in the holding area outside the operating room before surgery while she was still conscious. I had a copy of her patient record in my hand. I then asked her, as I always do, "What is the procedure we are doing today?" She, like most of my patients, gave me an incredulous look, as if I had forgotten our previous talks in my office or didn't know what I was to be doing. But I explained to her that I always ask this question to make absolutely certain I'm not making any mistakes.

The patient was taken into the operating room, and I went down the hall—outside the OR—to my locker, to remove my street clothes, undress to my undergarments, and put on the light-blue or light-green cotton scrub suit—the short-sleeve shirt and pants so familiar to television viewers who watch medical programs. I put on my scrub cap and mask and slipped booties on to cover my shoes.

Previously, the booties were worn to ensure that surgeons' bodies didn't create a ground that might allow a spark to jump through them and cause an explosion while using the electro-cautery machine or inflammable anesthetic agents. The machines and anesthetics are better today, but we still wear the booties to prevent the transfer of microorganisms from our street shoes to the OR.

As I began the methodical scrubbing of my hands and arms, I thought about the procedure before me and what I might find. What surprises might await me? I reviewed the studies on her diagnoses in my head, reminding myself just how much I knew about the disease and the surgery I was to perform. Then I thought about the possible scenarios—what might go wrong, and how I would deal with any problems that might come up.

Scrub time is a good time for training, too, and because I always have medical students or residents participating in my operations, I typically go over the procedure I plan to follow with them in the scrub room and ask them questions about what to expect.

Primum non nocere, I always remind them: First do no harm. "We want to help this patient, cure her if we can," I told them. "But as we do that, let's try hard to avoid hurting her." It's not the lesson in Latin that's important, but I tell them to keep in mind the expressions *mea culpa*—"my fault"—and *res ipsa loquitur*—"the thing speaks for itself" or whatever happens in the operating room is ultimately the surgeon's responsibility.

Using surgical soap, I washed my hands and forearms up to the elbows over and over, scrubbing for five minutes—it used to be ten—to remove as many bacteria from my skin as I can, knowing I can never get them all. Then I rinsed off the soap, raising my hands and letting the water flow from the hands to the wrists to the forearms and down to the elbows, then into the sink below, never letting the water drip back down my arms or touch my hands. Holding my hands out in front, keeping them always above the waist, I entered the sterile area of the operating theater, where I got a sterile towel from the scrub nurse and used one corner of it to dry one hand, wiping toward the elbow, then flipped the towel and used the other corner to dry the other hand in the same way.

I have followed this ritual for decades, just as my colleagues do, for we have learned the critical importance of cleanliness in surgery particularly and the danger a tiny infection can pose if it strikes a patient weakened by disease and the trauma of an operation. After the scrub, I donned a sterile gown and gloves and entered the OR. The anesthesiologist had several machines at hand and medications labeled on a table nearby. The nurses had their instruments on tables pulled right into the operating field to be close at hand.

Finally ready, I approached the table and joined my colleagues: the anesthesiologist, the scrub nurse who hands me the instruments, and the circulating nurse who moves around the room to bring needed supplies and instruments to the scrub nurse. I had my students and interns scrub for the operation, even though they were primarily observers and assistants, unlike surgical residents, who participate more actively.

Nowadays, before a patient is put under by the anesthesiologist, the circulating nurse calls "time out." The time-out rule was instituted after reports of rare but inexcusable mistakes. The nurse announces the patient's name, the scheduled procedure, and the site of the surgery. Then the anesthesiologist and I agree that the nurse's information is correct before we proceed. That morning, however, following the protocol of the day, the patient was anesthetized, the circulating nurse prepped the site with antiseptic, and the scrub nurse, residents, and I draped the patient with sterile sheets, leaving only the area of incision exposed.

"My scalpel, please," I said, and the operation began. My team was so accustomed to working together that the scrub nurse usually knew which instrument I needed before I asked for it. I soon found that the growth in the woman's intestines was stuck to the bladder, presenting my surgical team with a difficult choice: should we remove part of the bladder or not? The urologist was in the OR with us, and he looked into the bladder with a cystoscope.

"I believe it's inflammation and not cancer," he said, but he couldn't be certain. It was up to me to decide what to do. If it was cancer and I cut through it, then I would be making a mistake that could spread the cancer throughout the peritoneal cavity, a potentially disastrous development. If it was just inflammation, then the bladder wouldn't have to come out. I could remove the primary source of the problem—the infection in the large intestine—and treat the inflammation with antibiotics. In all likelihood, given the latter scenario, the patient would make a full recovery in a short time. But if I found cancer in the large intestine, I would have to remove the lesion then and there, along with the part of the bladder that we believed was involved. I would have to be very careful to cut around the malignancy and leave clear margins of good tissue to make sure I got out all the cancer.

If I had to take the patient's whole bladder out, I thought, I would have to create an artificial bladder for her out of a portion of her small intestine, making an opening in the abdominal wall and using adhesive to attach a bag on the outside to collect her urine. The patient would have to wear a bag for the rest of her life. If I took that course I would try to remove only as much bladder as necessary, leaving a smaller bladder if possible, rather than creating a new one.

Having seen several patients with diverticulitis (inflammation of balloon-like out-pouchings, usually involving the large intestine) with marked inflammatory changes, I began looking in the patient's abdomen for any thickening of surrounding structures while trying to determine if any of her nearby lymph nodes were enlarged or if there were abnormalities in her liver or peritoneal cavity that looked malignant. I didn't see any telltale grayish-white nodules suggesting cancer.

At that point, I was called upon to exercise my best judgment—that highly elusive, yet essential quality we surgeons employ when all the books, tests, and clinical findings just don't provide a clear roadmap. I call that the "Syphax moment," recalling my mentor's mastery of abdominal problems. That's the moment when the doctor must choose whether to play it safe and remove human tissue just because it *might* be deadly—and in the process change the patient's quality of life forever—or preserve as much tissue and function as possible, knowing that removing too little can result in a fatal return of the cancer. It's not a democratic decision-making process. The specialists around the patient tend to be a collegial group, offering their opinions and analysis and the benefit of their experience, but we don't take a vote. In the end, I, the attending surgeon, had to make the choice and act on it.

I decided that in all likelihood this patient had diverticulitis. So I carefully placed my scalpel between the mass in her colon and her bladder, and I began cutting away the colon tissue containing the suspicious mass. I didn't remove any of her bladder.

I immediately sent the specimen to the pathology lab and waited for a quick reading of the tissue, known as a frozen section, while the patient was still on the table. While my colleagues and I were waiting, the scrub nurse noticed that one of the pads we had placed in the abdominal cavity to hold the organs out of the way while we worked had a bit more blood on it

Family members surround 1955 picture of the author as a young surgeon: Top row—father LaSalle Doheny Leffall Sr., c. 1928, mother Martha Lula (Jordan) Leffall, c. 1950; 2nd row—5-year-old Leffall, who later skipped second grade and graduated high school at age 15; a 1940 "School Days" picture (age 10); Bottom row—with mother and sister Dolores C. Leffall, Ph. D., c. 1993.

Center: Courtesy, Howard University College of Medicine; All Others: Courtesy, LaSalle D. Leffall Jr.

Dr. William H. Gray Jr. (center), FAMC President during the author's college years; and four esteemed FAMC faculty and mentors, clockwise fr. left to right: Crawford B. Lindsay (English), Charity Mance (psychology); Russell Anderson (physiology), and Ethan Earl Ware (biology).

Photo of Dr. Gray: Courtesy, William H. Gray III; Photos of Lindsay, Mance, and Ware: Courtesy, Florida A&M University; Photo of Anderson: Courtesy, Howard University College of Medicine

The author (3rd fr. right, 1st row, kneeling) with fellow Sphinxmen of Alpha Phi Alpha Fraternity, Florida Agricultural & Mechanical College (FAMC) Beta Nu chapter, 1946. Julian "Cannonball" Adderley is 3rd fr. Left, kneeling; roommate George Rawls is 3rd fr. right, standing; and local crooner William Dandy is 2nd fr. Right, kneeling

Courtesy, Florida A&M University

The Howard University College of Medicine (HUCM) Class of 1952. Dr. Leffall is pictured 2nd row fr. bottom, 3rd fr. right.

Courtesy, Howard University College of Medicine

Three of Dr. Leffall's HUCM mentors, eminent physicians all: Dr. Joseph L. Johnson, Dean; Dr. Charles R. Drew, Chief of Surgery and noted blood preservation pioneer; and Dr. W. Montague Cobb, Professor of Anatomy and a leader in the movement to integrate Washington, D.C.'s hospitals.

Courtesy, Howard University College of Medicine

The 1958 Fellows of the Memorial Hospital for the Treatment of Cancer and Allied Diseases, known today as Memorial Sloan-Kettering Cancer Center. Dr. Leffall is 3rd row fr. top, 2nd fr. left.

Courtesy, LaSalle D. Leffall Jr.

After his father's death in 1951, the author received $500 for tuition and books from S&H Green Stamp fortune heir Walter Beinecke Jr. (right) to complete his final year of medical school; shown here in Nantucket with wife Katherine.

Courtesy, Betsy Shirley Michel

Newlyweds Dr. and Mrs. LaSalle and Ruthie (McWilliams) Leffall, August 1956.

Photograph by Clifton Cabell; Courtesy, LaSalle D. Leffall Jr.

Proud parents at son Donney's 1981 Harvard University graduation (Mrs. Leffall's mother, Mrs. Lillian McWilliams, is in the background).

Courtesy, LaSalle D. Leffall Jr.

Dr. Leffall is reunited in 1973 with former Freedmen's Hospital surgical resident Dr. Bernard L. Gipson, who assisted him with one of his first surgical procedures.

Courtesy, Howard University College of Medicine

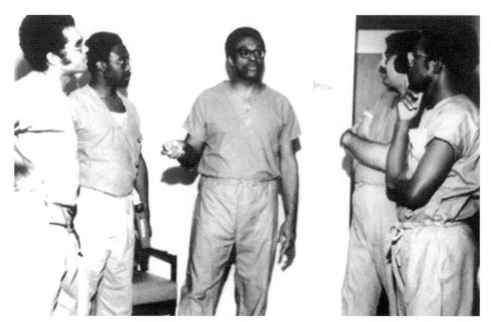

Dr. Leffall talks with residents outside the OR prior to a surgery. Left to right: Cecil Aird, Halstead Howell, Clarence Greene Jr., and John Hibbert.

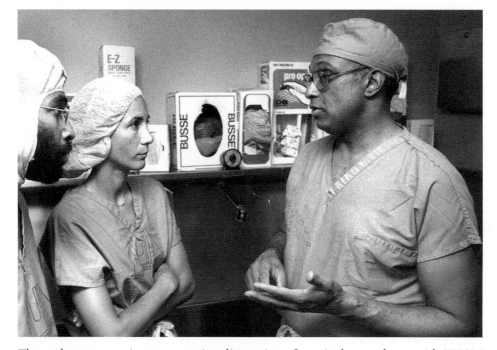

The author engages in pre-operative discussion of surgical procedures with HUCM students Nancy Santanello and Andrew Levette Jr.

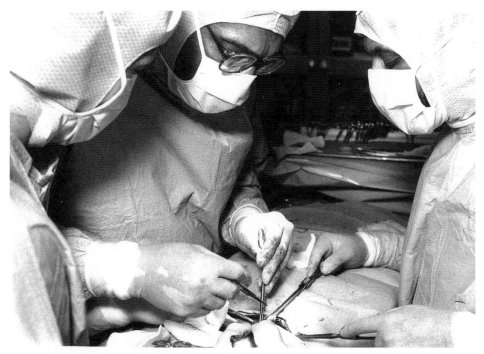

Dr. Leffall and his surgical team at work.
Courtesy, Howard University College of Medicine

Three of Dr. Leffall's esteemed HUCM colleagues and friends: Dr. Burke "Mickey" Syphax, Chair of the Department of Surgery from 1957 to 1970; Dr. Jack E. White, first African American trained as a cancer surgeon at Memorial Sloan-Kettering and founder of the Howard University Cancer Center; and Dr. Clive O Callender, a leader in minority organ transplantation, who succeeded Leffall as Chair of the Department of Surgery in 1996.
Courtesy, Howard University College of Medicine

The surgeon contemplating one of his instruments . . .
Courtesy, Jeffrey Henson Scales

. . . and longtime friend and jazz master Julian "Cannonball" Adderley, contemplating his instrument during a recording session in New York City, 1958.
Courtesy, Milton J. Hinton©

than she thought was normal. She pointed out the spot, and sure enough, we found bleeding from a small blood vessel underneath the pad.

I like to think that I would have spotted this problem and fixed it myself before we finished, but the nurse's input reminded me how valuable it is to have more than one pair of eyes on a patient at all times. An experienced team—comprised of an anesthesiologist, skilled nurses, and assorted less visible but equally valuable technicians in supporting roles—is critical to the success of any surgeon, who tends to get all the credit in the OR.

The importance of each person in the OR has become more apparent to all of us in the surgery field in recent years as patient safety has emerged as a watchword. New procedures, such as the "time out," have been instrumental in focusing the whole team's attention on the job at hand.

The report from pathology came back negative a few minutes later: there was no indication of cancer. The tension in the room dropped, and with great relief we rejoined the ends of the patient's large intestine, closed her abdominal cavity, and hooked her up to intravenous antibiotics to clear up her inflammation.

If the pathologist had told us I had made a mistake and that the lesion was cancerous, we all would have changed our gloves and instruments just to make sure we wouldn't spread any lingering bad tissue back into the abdominal cavity, then gone back in and removed any suspicious area that might contain malignant cells. We would have sent those tissues out for a frozen section test as well.

Unfortunately, I don't often get such encouraging results. There are many times when I can't even offer a patient the slightest chance for a cure. But I always try to offer them hope. When the news is not good, I tell my patients that with the current state of knowledge, I cannot cure them, but I can help them. I can treat the pain, I tell them, and while I am doing that, somebody may be doing some work at the National Institutes of

Health or some other research facility that may provide a cure for what they have.

Patients can usually relate to that. I can't say they will live longer, but the quality of the life they will have as a result will be unquestionably enhanced. I call that "realistic hope."

When I know I'm dealing with cancer beforehand, I wait until my patient is recovered enough from the effects of anesthesia after surgery when they can fully understand what I am saying. I try to arrange for the patient's spouse or closest relative to be there to listen as well. Sometimes that's the first day; sometimes not until the third, depending on the pace of recovery. Then I give the patient a preliminary report of my findings, based on the operation and the early lab results. I don't make a final decision until I see the full pathology report, which is usually available three to four days after surgery.

At the first opportunity I meet with the patient to go over the findings again. I always try to use a comforting, upbeat tone. I try to avoid saying, "Don't worry about it; we'll take care of it." I do try to be realistic and hopeful at the same time. Some patients accept bad news very well. Others break down in my office. Some break down later, others not at all. I've found no way to predict a patient's reaction.

This time I was able to tell my patient, "I have good news for you." When I explained we had determined her problem was caused by inflammation and not cancer, she broke out in tears of joy.

"I prayed, Dr. Leffall. I prayed, and God answered my prayers. I can now get on to my *real* life."

I said my own silent prayer of thanks, too.

9

Leadership Lessons Learned:
My Years at the American Cancer Society

The American Society for the Control of Cancer was formed in 1913 and reorganized in 1946 as the American Cancer Society. The society is the largest voluntary cancer organization in the world with over three million professional and lay volunteers. The society has programs in prevention, screening, diagnosis, treatment, and rehabilitation. Further, it supports a broad range of research, professorships, and public and professional education programs. It was among the first organizations to support efforts addressing cancer health disparities.

During my fellowship at Sloan-Kettering in New York, colleagues advised us budding cancer surgeons to join the local affiliates of the American Cancer Society where we planned to practice. To me, this seemed like a great opportunity to extend my work with cancer in the operating room to preventing the disease itself. Soon after I returned to Howard in 1962 following my military service, I signed up as a member of the District of Columbia division of the society. My career with the organization almost ended before it began, however.

At Howard, we were already sensitive to high cancer rates among blacks, although we didn't yet have statistics to back us up. I believed cancer education programs aimed at the black community could help. Membership in a voluntary organization such as the American Cancer Society also seemed consistent with my father's guidance to dedicate some of my time and talents to helping my community, not just earning a living. Several people I knew at Howard's medical school were already members, and I had other colleagues and friends around town who had joined the group. It seemed a natural step.

At one of the first ACS meetings I attended, I was appointed to a committee assigned to develop a cancer-control initiative in a low-income area of the city where the disease was prevalent. I dived in headfirst. My fellow committee members and I spent long hours researching the issues, debating alternatives, and drawing up a plan to enlist local churches, schools, and fraternal and service organizations in cancer-screening programs aimed at our target neighborhoods. When we were ready, the committee chair presented our plan at a monthly meeting of the society and we got turned down—flat. The senior members of the division simply dismissed our proposal, tabled any discussion of it at the meeting, and moved on to other topics without so much as a second thought!

I could hardly believe it! I immediately demanded the floor and threatened to resign from the division on the spot if our committee's ideas weren't given consideration. The veterans didn't budge. I stormed out of the room with no intention of ever going back. I had a rather good reputation by that time, and I wasn't accustomed to having my ideas turned down without so much as a tip of the hat.

Later that day Dr. Robert Jason, my one-time pathology professor who was then dean of the med school, came by my office and told me he'd heard about my temper tantrum at the meeting. I had cooled off a bit since then and was able to explain what had happened in a less strident tone, but I was still upset and feeling that I had been rudely slighted. Dr. Jason listened patiently, then told me calmly that I had really failed to see the big picture.

The District division, he said, was preoccupied with some financial difficulties and was in no position to deal with any new initiatives at the moment. "Don't make any hasty decisions," he advised. "You can wield much more influence inside the organization than outside."

I agreed to stay, secretly relieved to be given a second chance. We eventually got our plan through, and in the next four decades, I saw firsthand that the American Cancer Society has done more than perhaps any other organization in the world to raise awareness in minority and poor communities about their residents' special vulnerability to cancer and what they can do about it. I'm proud of my part in sponsoring such programs, from the floor and as president of both the Washington, D.C. division and the national organization in the 1970s. Had it not been for Dean Jason, my youthful arrogance could have cost me one of the most important roles of my career. I came that close to denying myself an extraordinary opportunity to serve.

I did return to the next local ACS meeting, and the plan I had helped develop was eventually adopted. My first assignment from Joseph Leverenz, then executive vice president of the division, was to try to reach out to the black community.

Soon afterwards a member of my neighborhood's Community Involvement Committee invited me to come talk to her church group about screening and diagnosis. About thirty people showed up for the meeting. Recalling Morehouse College president Benjamin Mays's remark that "speaking from notes is like kissing a beautiful young lady—over the telephone," I practiced giving my talk without a written text, something I have tried to do ever since college. I prefer to speak from the heart, rarely referring to a script when speaking before lay groups. My college debate team days were good training for what has become a forty-year career in public speaking that I have sandwiched in between my "routine" of seeing patients, operating, and teaching. When making presentations before professional groups, I often use slides.

I am often asked how I mastered the internal politics of organizations such as the American Cancer Society and how much, if any, I believed all my "outside" activities took away from my career as teacher and surgeon. I confess I have always been a man of ambition, and somewhere along the way I realized I too might attain higher office, not only in the ACS but also in various other professional groups. I did not, however, campaign for any position. Besides, you simply cannot *campaign* for the presidency of the American Cancer Society! It just doesn't work that way.

Nor have I used politics to get ahead. Instead, my abiding rule of thumb, given any assignment, has simply been to do my job and do it well. Then, when names are being considered for a higher-up position, the likelihood that mine would come up is automatically increased. For me, it's been just like my mentor Charles Drew said it would be: "Excellence of performance will transcend artificial barriers created by man."

I acknowledge, however, that there have been instances when my hard work simply wasn't good enough; when other factors, either race or something else, got in the way. But those instances only made me more determined to succeed the next time.

Unlike the various medical and professional groups I joined, the American Cancer Society has always had a substantial number of lay people in its leadership as well as health care professionals like me. The professionals tend to be specialists in cancer research or treatment, but frequently lay people get involved in that aspect too because they have watched a friend or family member struggle with the disease. When I learned how committed the ACS leadership was to fighting cancer, I realized that I too could just as easily get caught up in the fervor of that battle.

If this one organization could help people understand the causes of cancer, how to avoid contracting the disease, and how to detect it early, I knew that I could save many more lives working with it than I could alone with my knife, no matter how good a surgeon I was.

I had been working with the D.C. division of the society for several years when I was asked to be delegate-at-large to the national body. It was 1970, and the ACS wanted to reach people it had not been able to get to with its traditional methods. That, of course, included minorities, to whom I had devoted much of my efforts. I was elected president of the D.C. division from 1974 to 1976, and I guess the folks at the national level noticed me. In 1977 I was selected by the nominating committee of the national board to serve a year as president-elect, then take over as president the following year. The job meant I would be traveling extensively to speak at various conferences and meet hundreds of volunteers.

My colleagues at Howard agreed to help me fulfill my commitments to my private-practice patients so that I could take on the added responsibilities. I was so grateful for their help because I frequently had to tell my patients that although I would be the surgeon operating on them, my colleagues would have to look after them in the post-operative period.

In November 1978, Ruthie, Donney, and several friends from Washington came to New York City for my installation as ACS president. I invited my mother to join us from Quincy, and I arranged for her to stay with us at the posh Waldorf-Astoria Hotel as my honored guest. There she was showered with a level of elegance unknown in my hometown. Mother wasn't a person easily swayed by pomp, but she was pretty impressed by the beautiful cut flowers in her room, the luxurious appointments, the marble bathroom, and the crystal chandeliers. The closets, she noted, were the size of motel rooms elsewhere, and the ceilings were high overhead.

Before the ceremony, I took her to lunch in the hotel's dining room—just the two of us—and we naturally started telling stories about my father.

"Wouldn't Daddy be proud if he could be here today?" she remarked. "You're the first black person to be president of the American Cancer Society, coming from the little town of Quincy."

Then she reminded me that it wasn't all my own doing. "If you hadn't listened to your father and me over the years," she said, "this never would have happened."

"He was right," she added with a smile, "'With a good education and hard work, combined with honesty and integrity, there are no boundaries.'"

In the crowded dining room of the Waldorf-Astoria, she and I paused and shared a moment of contented silence.

I wanted the hallmark of my ACS presidency to be a national conference focusing on the disturbing disparities in cancer prevalence, treatment, and mortality between white and black Americans. The idea grew out of the landmark study my colleagues and I had published six years earlier documenting blacks' disproportionate cancer death rates, especially from prostate, lung, and colorectal cancers. Easier said than done, I soon realized.

Some members of the executive committee argued that we shouldn't single out any one group for special attention. Others claimed the evidence was insufficient to justify a conference focusing solely on blacks. Up to that time most ACS conferences had been dedicated to a single area such as screening or diagnosis, treatment or rehabilitation, and no one group of people had been singled out for special attention.

Lane Adams, the society's executive vice president and a skillful negotiator, and Dr. Arthur Holleb, its chief medical officer who had been my mentor at Sloan-Kettering, joined me in the quiet battle to do it our way. We argued that the proposed conference would not only raise awareness among blacks but would serve as a prototype for getting cancer information to all racial and ethnic minority groups. In addition, it would help ACS target other medically underserved population groups, including whites, especially in rural America.

We carried the day, and I worked diligently to make sure no one would be sorry for staging what became the "National Conference on Meeting the Challenge of Cancer among Black Americans," held in Washington, D.C., in February 1979.

I milked my contacts to the bone to draw speakers I knew could capture the attention of a wide audience in the African-American community. One was the talented and beautiful Lena Horne, whose classic recordings of "Stormy Weather" and "Just One of Those Things" had made her name a household word in black America. Horne had proved her mettle when she became the first black actor to sign a major Hollywood studio contract, and she had risen above the stereotypical servant roles generally given to blacks to achieve true stardom as a respected and versatile actress. She agreed to serve as honorary chairperson of our conference and threw her unstinting support into planning the watershed event. Vernon Jordan, then president of the National Urban League, agreed to give what turned out to be a stirring keynote address about the problems facing black Americans. He pledged the Urban League's support around the country to educate communities about the special problems the ACS had identified.

My team and I assembled an array of black researchers, physicians, community educators, health advocates, cancer specialists, and survivors to draw participants to the conference. The meeting's sessions emphasized the increased incidence of prostate, lung, and colorectal cancer among blacks. Several pointed out that although breast cancer was more common among whites, it was growing in prevalence among blacks—and killing them at a higher rate. Presentations examined several socioeconomic factors, including poverty, lack of health insurance coverage, and unemployment, as reasons why cancer tended to be diagnosed later in blacks and therefore was more often fatal. Panel discussions explored the latest research and focused on how blacks could make lifestyle changes that would improve their chances of survival.

Smokers and the tobacco companies weren't on the defensive then as they are today, of course, but our meeting presented studies informing people that at least one third of all human cancers are caused by tobacco use. Speakers talked about how high-fiber, reduced-fat diets and exercise can help prevent cancer and improve cure rates. Many people, especially those in poor neighborhoods without the benefit of good education and regular health care, didn't know then how important it was for women to get regular Pap smears to detect cancer of the cervix and mammograms to spot abnormalities in breast tissue that can lead to cancer—but they were informed of that at our conference. They also learned why doctors should perform a digital rectal exam to identify signs of an enlarged prostate. (That was a few years before development of the blood test for prostate specific antigen—PSA—a more reliable way to check for prostate cancer.)

A simple test of a stool sample can pick up signs of blood in feces, often an indicator of colon cancer, and more sophisticated—but still routine—examinations known as sigmoidoscopy or colonoscopy can be used to spot cancerous or precancerous polyps before they grow into potentially deadly lesions. Most African-Americans weren't aware of that. To get the word out, speakers urged those who came to the conference to go home and visit their schools, churches, medical societies, and service and fraternal organizations to share what they had learned. They were also asked to lobby lawmakers at every level to increase funding for cancer research and cancer control.

At the conclusion of this now historic conference I told the gathered audience, "We know there is much to be done. It will not end with the publication of the proceedings of this conference. There can be no substitute for our actions. We believe our cause is just, our charge is real, our commitment is true, our course is set. There can be no turning back."

That conference helped to change the way people think about cancer, race and reaching people in underserved areas. I am proud to know that I helped plant the seeds that later grew into dozens of innovative and effective programs aimed at specific groups around the nation and the world. These include the Healthy Women Partnership in New York City and the New Jersey Cancer Education and Early Detection Program; Let's Talk About It, a program focusing on black men and their increased risk of prostate cancer; Man to Man/Brother to Brother, which provides confidential links between African- American prostate cancer survivors and those newly diagnosed with the disease; and Sister to Sister, a breast cancer program aimed at black women. The American Cancer Society has since developed English/Spanish initiatives and reached out to South Asian Americans and other racial and ethnic minorities in the U.S. and abroad.

One physician on our conference organizing committee, Dr. Harold Freeman, had been one of my first students at Howard Med. He was a junior medical student when I was chief surgical resident, and we discovered we had a common interest in jazz. Harold liked the Modern Jazz Quartet, and he and I often had friendly arguments over who played better—the Adderleys or the MJQ. Like me, he became a surgeon, and he followed my footsteps from Howard to Memorial Sloan-Kettering. After the "Challenge" conference, Freeman returned to his position at Harlem Hospital in New York determined to focus on the relationship between cancer, race, and poverty. He rose to chief of surgery at Harlem, retained his special commitment to the poor, and was himself elected president of the American Cancer Society ten years after my term.

The society's concern prompted other organizations to launch similar initiatives. Freeman currently heads the National Cancer Institute's Center to Reduce Cancer Health Disparities.

Louis Sullivan, later secretary of Health and Human Services, was a member of the National Cancer Advisory Board and was one of the leaders of the National Black Leadership Initiative on Cancer.

Two scientists in Texas, Dr. Lovell Jones of M. D. Anderson Cancer Center, and Dr. Armin Weinberg at Baylor College of Medicine later started a biannual conference to keep the focus on the unequal burden of cancer among different ethnic groups. They grew that effort into the Intercultural Cancer Council, whose goal is to ensure all people have access to care. Dr. Jones also heads the Center for Research for Minority Health.

Today almost all cancer prevention programs in the United States have targeted programs aimed at minorities and the poor, but we still have a long way to go. Only half the blacks who get cancer today will survive five years compared to 60 percent of whites. But consider how far we've come! When I became a cancer surgeon, only about 40 percent of all cancer patients survived. We didn't even have *statistics* on blacks then. Blacks today still have the highest incidence of lung and colorectal cancer among U.S. ethnic groups and also the highest death rate from colorectal cancer—primarily because they are not screened as frequently as other populations and their tumors aren't caught in time. And for reasons that remain a mystery, black men in this country are 50 percent more likely to develop prostate cancer than are other men.

We know it's not just due to insufficient screening. Researchers are looking at environmental factors, genetics, and diet, all of which may contribute to the wide disparity. We also know that black Americans have a much higher incidence than black Africans, whose rate is lower than that of white Americans, but we don't have conclusive studies to tell us why.

Many questions like this have arisen as a result of the ACS's nearly thirty years of focus on different racial and ethnic groups and on the varying statistics for populations in other parts of the world. These questions have prompted researchers to recruit more blacks for clinical trials in cancer research and to name minority researchers to help design and direct those trials.

During my two years as president-elect and then president of the American Cancer Society, I traveled extensively to rally the troops and update local organizations on new research findings. In Washington, D.C., I lobbied Congress to increase funding for National Cancer Institute research projects. On one sentimental journey, I returned to Huntsville, Alabama, the place where I had spent every Saturday for eleven summers of my childhood when I visited my mother's family in Maysville, just outside that city. My mother and her twin brother Harris greeted me on my ACS trip, along with scores of other relatives who still lived nearby. Maynard Layman, the chairman of the Madison County unit of the society, which I was to address that day, had played baseball with my Uncle Harris as a boy. It was the only time Uncle Harris ever heard me speak at a cancer program, but during my childhood summers in Alabama, it was he who stimulated me to do more reading. He taught me much about Civil War history.

On many of my trips to local division meetings I was accompanied by a patient, Mr. Henry Spencer, who allowed me to demonstrate the life-changing strides medical professionals could make by combining the expertise of very different specialties. During my talk, I would invite Spencer to come up on stage with me, and I would ask him how he was feeling. He responded with such a severe nasal impediment that the audience couldn't understand what he was saying. There was inevitably a moment of evident discomfort among those watching and wondering why I would ask someone to speak who had such a severe defect. Then Spencer would reach into his pocket, take out a small prosthesis, and slip it onto the roof of his mouth. His voice instantly became crystal clear, and he would chat with me on stage with no indication whatsoever that his speech had been so seriously impaired.

Afterward I would explain to the audience that Spencer had been suffering from cancer of the hard palate, and that I had saved his life by removing the tumor but the surgery had left him with a debilitating hole in his palate. I then would tell them that I had asked specialists at the Howard University College of Dentistry if they could make a "plug" to close the space between his mouth and his sinuses. Our interdisciplinary teamwork was so successful, I explained, that my patient became an ardent Cancer Society volunteer, traveling around the country with me to demonstrate the success of his treatment and the hope his recovery could give to others. Spencer ended his appearance by singing a beautiful and moving rendition of the Lord's Prayer.

While I was head of the society it cosponsored a program with United Way of America emphasizing early screening and diagnosis. As a result of that relationship I was invited to join the board of United Way and became chairman of its Executive Committee in 1990. That experience actually turned out to be one of the greatest tests of my credo to maintain "equanimity under duress."

It was a volunteer job but, of course, my fellow board members and I shared responsibility for overseeing the widely respected charitable organization with more than a thousand local chapters. We were as shocked as everyone else when we discovered that our gifted $400,000-a-year president and CEO had misappropriated contributed funds and converted them to his own use. The scandal ignited a firestorm in the press, which questioned how the organization had handled millions of dollars collected largely from small donors via payroll deduction programs at work. Throughout the CEO's initial denials and the spreading federal investigation, I was pounded with questions and hounded by the media to explain what had happened. I didn't know exactly, but I had one guideline I followed throughout: tell the truth.

As the tale of internal corruption unraveled, I was shocked at many of the revelations, but I was absolutely certain that I had never benefited financially from anything that had been done and that we would eventually get to the bottom of it. The CEO went to prison, and all of us on the board got a tough lesson in the importance of doing our own homework, no matter how good the staff seems to be. We were, ultimately, responsible for what had happened. *Mea culpa.*

The most rewarding part of my career with the society was working with volunteers whose own struggle with cancer tapped a wellspring of courage and self-sacrifice that more fortunate people may never find within themselves. A few years after I started giving time to the society I began working with a cancer patient who used her encounter with the disease to support and inspire others around the world. Her name was Marvella Bayh, wife of then-Senator Birch Bayh and mother of Senator Evan Bayh of Indiana. Marvella was diagnosed with breast cancer in 1971, but she underwent surgery and was doing well when I got to know her through our mutual work for the society.

Marvella had an incredible will to live—not just for herself but for her family, friends, and others living with cancer. She and I traveled the country together many times to appear at ACS events, frequently alternating with one of us giving the luncheon speech and the other speaking at dinner.

In those days, more than now, people who survived five years without a recurrence of their cancer were thought of as cured, and I remember Marvella called me one day to say that it was the fifth anniversary of her surgery, and she and Birch were going out to celebrate. Eighteen months later, however, her doctors discovered that her malignancy had returned and spread to her bones. Before long, she was thin and frail, but with steely determination she kept up her busy schedule, exuding the most enthusiastic, positive attitude imaginable.

Marvella succumbed to cancer on April 24, 1979. She was only forty-six. Throughout her struggle, I never saw her show a single sign of self-pity. She taught everyone who encountered her how to be strong and resilient. To Marvella, life was worth fighting for—right to the end.

When she died I issued a statement as president of the society saying that after her breast cancer operation, "She found within herself a new sense of determination, a zest for life that sparked confidence and hope . . . She transmitted strength to women all over the country as she spoke to them, visited them at the bedside and answered their letters and calls."

At her memorial services at the National Cathedral in Washington, D.C., and in Terre Haute, Indiana, I shared with her mourners a story about my late friend Cannonball Adderley, who came to visit me in Washington many years earlier and how he and I were in my den listening to John Coltrane's "Lush Life." As "Trane's" saxophone solo grew really intense, I recalled, Cannonball closed his eyes, lifted his huge arms over his shoulders, and raised his hands toward the ceiling. He stood there transfixed, I told them, as if in prayer—head down, a beatific smile on his face. "I knew he was in that zone musicians enter when all the music they ever heard or dreamed about comes together in one smooth, all-encompassing rendition," I said. Still smiling, Cannonball turned to me and asked: "How'd you like that grace note, frat brother?"

I told the crowd I must have looked perplexed because Cannonball laughed and grabbed me around the shoulders. "Well, you're not a musician, are you, LaSalle?" he said. "And you probably couldn't know what a grace note is!"

I admitted I didn't have a clue what he was talking about.

I explained that Cannonball then fell back into his easy chair and broke it down for me:

"A grace note," he said, "is a note whose timing doesn't affect the rhythm of the bar. It's just something a little . . . extra . . . like an ornament." I told them that a smile crept across my friend's great face. "When you hear something really beautiful, man," he said, "it's often a grace note."

Marvella, I said in closing, filled our lives with grace notes.

During my years with the American Cancer Society, I met many volunteers like Marvella Bayh who gave every drop of energy they had to help others cope with a dreadful disease. After speaking at a division dinner one night, I was introduced to a man who was regarded as one of the region's best volunteers. "You want to know why I'm so involved in the society's work, Dr. Leffall?" the man asked, grasping my hand in a firm handshake. "Let me tell you."

"A few years ago, I had just two ambitions in life. One was to make as much money as I could because I was a very poor boy growing up and was driven to succeed. I was a ruthless man, but I achieved my goal. I got married, and my wife and I had a son, our only child. My second ambition was to give my son all the things I never had: toys, cars, clothes, camp, trips, the best schools, everything. I could afford it, and I did."

The volunteer's voice weakened and cracked, but he forged ahead, still holding my hand: "My son died of cancer as a teenager. His mother and I were devastated. I didn't want to live. But after his death, people I never even knew came to help us. They were kind and understanding. They went out of their way to see that we made it through our loss. I didn't believe people could be that way."

His intense brown eyes took on a wistful look as he added, "I've often wondered if I had ever been unkind to any of those people who were so good to me. I'll never know the answer to that one, but I know now what life is really all about: Giving back! I'm sorry that my son is no longer here to share that wonderful knowledge with me."

I thought to myself: what a remarkable gift that once-jaded man had gained from his terrible loss. He had turned his life around and was finally able to take personal satisfaction from helping those who needed more than his money. They needed what others had given him: a passage through pain.

When I joined the society's board in 1970, I became friends with a fellow director named Eppie Lederer, better known to the world as the advice columnist Ann Landers. Eppie's column appeared in over a thousand daily newspapers with a readership of about ninety million in those days, making her one of the most influential women in America. Her pithy, common-sense instructions to the lovelorn, the bewildered, and the frightened were often bolstered by the authority of good reporting. She never hesitated to seek the counsel of experts when the matter was important.

Cancer was one of the issues she considered top priority, and I became accustomed to her many probing inquiries. We spoke frequently and served together again several years later when President Jimmy Carter named both of us to the National Cancer Advisory Board serving from 1980 to 1986. In 1990 a woman lamented in her letter to Ann Landers that her doctor had misdiagnosed her breast cancer as a benign cyst, and Eppie quoted me in her column advising women that a biopsy is mandatory if a self-exam or mammogram reveals a solid lump in a breast.

"Clip this column and read it again the next time you go for a mammogram," Eppie wrote. "If your doctor doesn't follow the procedure outlined by Dr. Leffall, hand it to him or her."

Eppie remained a friend and an influential advocate of cancer detection and treatment for many years. Once she plugged a book called *Fighting Cancer* in her column, and the next day the R. A. Bloch Cancer Foundation in Kansas City, which published the book, was swamped by more than 400,000 attempts to call its toll-free phone number.

However, when she herself was diagnosed in early 2002 with a bone marrow cancer called multiple myeloma, Eppie didn't call me or other friends in the cancer community. She chose to keep working, writing her column as long as she could without telling anyone of her illness. "Ann Landers" died June 22, 2002. She was eighty-three.

Years after I met Eppie, I helped recruit a couple of other volunteers from the nonmedical community. In 1998 John Seffrin and Harmon Eyre of the American Cancer Society, Andrew von Eschenbach of the M. D. Anderson Cancer Center at the University of Texas, and I traveled to Kennebunkport, Maine, to meet with former President George H. W. Bush and his wife Barbara. Von Eschenbach, a nationally recognized urologic oncologist who later was named director of the National Cancer Institute, introduced us to the Bushes because we were looking for people with clout to bring together the nation's many disparate voices on cancer for an ongoing dialogue on how to eradicate the disease as a major health problem. As a young couple, the Bushes had lost a daughter to acute leukemia when she was not quite four-years-old. That was in 1953, when there was no cure for that form of cancer, and they have been active in cancer awareness and control programs ever since.

There are many well-meaning people and organizations, of course. Some focus on research, others on treatment; some choose to educate the public about early detection, others to help patients and their families get through the hard times. Those who have suffered from breast cancer or who know others who do may want to pour their energies into combating that particular form of the disease. All, of course, need money, and fundraising is a critical part of most charitable work. Government agencies, pharmaceutical companies, medical centers and academic institutions all play influential roles in waging war against the disease. Seffrin, Eyre, von Eschenbach, and I wanted to bring the many strong-willed leaders in all those organizations together for a continuing discussion of progress, priorities, and needs. We were convinced that the Bushes were dedicated enough in the fight against cancer to help us.

We presented our concept to the former President and First Lady and urged them to take part. They listened intently but expressed concerns that their involvement would be seen as a political ploy. We countered that their personal stake in the fight against cancer easily overcame any political criticism. And then we reminded them how far we'd come in that battle. Forty-five years after their daughter's death, we reminded them, children born with leukemia have a greater than 80 percent chance of being cured and growing up to live normal lives. That is one measure of the progress we've made.

The Bushes agreed to serve as leadership cochairs of what we decided to call the National Dialogue on Cancer, known today as C-Change. I chair the organization's board of directors. C-Change has assembled more than 130 collaborating partners, with much of the credit for that success going to the Bushes. Its vice chair, Senator Dianne Feinstein of California—who has lost a husband, father, and several friends to cancer—has also been a powerful voice in C-Change. Our group works to encourage prevention, promote legislative measures to curb tobacco use, develop state cancer plans, expand cancer research and ensure access to high-quality cancer care.

The American Cancer Society's Committee on the Worldwide Fight Against Cancer maintains liaison with cancer organizations throughout the world and arranges visits to different countries to share and exchange information. With a group of cancer specialists, I was granted permission to travel on an ACS mission to Communist countries when such travel was unusual except for government delegations. This reflects the universality of medicine and how it can transcend politics and be used to establish closer ties between countries—in our case the fight against cancer. Our hosts showed us great courtesy and hospitality.

In all of the countries we visited, there was a common theme: to learn as much as we could about prevention, diagnosis, and treatment of cancer in order to help patients. In our discussions worldwide, the patient always came first and assumed the role of primacy.

I was a member of ACS fact-finding missions in the late 1970s to assess needs in far-flung places such as Russia and Ukraine during the Soviet period. I also joined delegations to China and Liberia, and I was among the first Americans to go to Vietnam after the war. One group traveled in Beijing a year after the death of Chairman Mao Tse-tung, the communist revolutionary, and we spent six weeks visiting treatment centers, specialists, and cancer programs around the People's Republic. We were delighted to learn that ACS's own journal, *Ca: A Cancer Journal for Clinicians*, was one of the major sources of information about cancer for Chinese physicians and cancer specialists. That nation's revolutionary government had sent nearly two million "barefoot doctors" and "Red medical workers" into the countryside decades before to provide health care and teach preventive techniques—with remarkable success.

It was discouraging, though, that when our delegation would sit down with our Chinese counterparts in one city after another, we would invariably find packs of cigarettes on the table, and our hosts would quickly light up before we even began to talk. Imagine our angst: there we were, sitting around a long conference table discussing cancer prevention through a haze of cigarette smoke! We tried to raise that issue as politely as we could, given that we were guests in their country, but our Chinese colleagues simply told us that both Chairman Mao and Premier Chou En-lai had been heavy smokers all their lives and both lived to be old men. So our hosts went right on puffing away.

I found that we in the West had much to learn from Eastern medicine—and we still do. The Chinese were performing lung resections, thyroidectomies, and colon resections using acupuncture instead of anesthesia. I watched in awe as one patient, after a two-hour lung operation, sat up, smiled at us and said she felt quite well, despite the tubes still protruding from her chest! Western medicine has not explained the remarkable effects of acupuncture, but there was no denying that it worked for that patient.

Our trip disclosed another curiosity that perplexed our hosts, as well as our delegation. The people of Linhsien County in northern China were experiencing a high incidence of cancer of the esophagus. Even their chickens were developing cancer of the gullet and upper gastrointestinal tract. Our Chinese colleagues told us the phenomenon had not been seen elsewhere. We had to agree. They thought it might be related to the presence of nitrosamines (cancer-producing substances) and fungi in the local food and low amounts of molybdenum in the soil. Some Western scientific studies followed, but the exact causes remain elusive to this day.

One of the delegates on that China trip was a woman whose background was as different from mine as I could imagine. Her name was Egie Huff, and she came from a well-to-do white family in Rome, a small southern city in the heart of Georgia. Egie was a tall woman, maybe 5 feet 11, with a lovely face and beautiful smile. She and I were both products of a segregated society, and in our youth our paths never would have crossed. We met in 1970 when I joined the national board of the society, of which she already was a member. By the time we went to China, she was vice chairman of the board and a tireless worker in the society's behalf. Eating breakfast, lunch, and dinner together every day for six weeks on that trip, we became close friends. Later, when she contracted ovarian cancer, we kept in touch by phone every two or three weeks as she battled her disease.

When Egie lost her fight with cancer after several years, her family asked me to come to Rome to speak at her memorial service. Of course, I did, and in my eulogy I recalled our special relationship as friends from different worlds, brought together by a common cause. Egie had a sense of civility, I noted, a natural tendency toward tolerance and understanding that overcame the culture into which she was born. I will always miss her warmth and the true friendship we shared.

In 1978, three years after the Vietnam War ended, Senator Edward M. Kennedy organized a five-person delegation to evaluate the health and humanitarian needs of our recent enemy. He asked me to join the group that included Dr. Jean Mayer, a nutrition expert and president of Tufts University; the Reverend Philip Hannan, archbishop of New Orleans; Mildred Kaufman, chair of the Food and Nutrition Section of the American Public

Health Association; and Jerry Tinker, a member of the senator's staff.

Life expectancy in Vietnam after the war was only fifty-eight years, and epidemic diseases such as diarrhea, tuberculosis, skin infections, and venereal diseases were common. About 40 percent of the population carried or suffered from malaria. Public health authorities reported increases in cardiovascular diseases and cancer. The Vietnamese Ministry of Health was struggling to increase the number of clinics, hospital beds, and physicians, but health care was so limited that the country of fifty million had only eight physicians for every ten thousand people. Medicines, supplies, and medical training of all types were in short supply.

As the surgeon in our group, I spent several hours with Professor Ton That Tung, the leading surgeon in Vietnam, who took me on rounds with him and shared his extensive experience with liver tumors. He had noted a sharp increase in the incidence of hepatomas (cancerous liver tumors), and although he didn't yet have scientific data to back it up, he concluded that the only logical explanation was the Americans' widespread aerial spraying of Agent Orange, a defoliant containing the highly toxic chemical dioxin, during the protracted war. I was impressed by his knowledge of liver tumors and how to treat them and believed his findings should not be ignored.

When our group left Southeast Asia, we were allowed to escort a group of twenty-nine Vietnamese mothers and children who were to be reunited with the American servicemen who had fathered the children during the war. As we stood on the tarmac at the Bangkok airport, a cute little brown-skinned girl ran right into my arms with a huge smile on her face. Her father was obviously a black GI, and as I held her I realized that she and I were perhaps the only people on the plane of African-American descent. Though mixed, she must have felt an instant bond.

The next year I led a delegation to Africa to evaluate cancer programs in Liberia, where cervical cancer was widespread but few women were aware that a simple test, the Pap smear, could save their lives. A former colleague at Sloan-Kettering, Dr. Nehemiah Cooper, was in charge of a state-of-the art surgical clinic in Monrovia, and I was delighted to be able to offer some support for his efforts. The delegation admired the work of Cooper and a number of other dedicated, well-educated health care providers we met in Liberia.

A year later, Liberian President William Tolbert, who had treated us like royalty, and several high-ranking Liberian officials were assassinated in a coup that threw the nation into chaos. Cooper was forced to close his clinic. Liberia has yet to recover, but I remain hopeful that the dedicated people I met during that visit will find a way to reestablish the foundation for good health care they worked so hard to establish. My experience in Liberia emphasized how closely linked the two are—a stable government and access to quality health care.

At home, the ACS scored a breakthrough with the U.S. government. The society had always been in the forefront of the fight against tobacco. The link between smoking and cancer was clear to its leadership long before it was acknowledged by state and federal authorities, who had to answer to the tobacco lobby, one of the most powerful special interests anyone could confront. Dr. Luther Terry braved the wrath of the tobacco industry, the tobacco states, and their representatives in 1964 when he issued the famous first Surgeon's General's Report on Smoking and Health. Fourteen years later, officials were still cautious about the mounting evidence identifying tobacco as a mass killer.

In January 1978, working with the ACS and other groups such as the American Heart Association and American Lung Association, U.S. Secretary of Health, Education, and Welfare Joseph A. Califano, Jr., created a National Council on Smoking and Health and declared cigarette smoking "Public Health

Enemy No. 1" in the United States. A former heavy smoker who struggled to quit at the request of his eleven-year-old son, Califano later founded the Center on Addiction and Substance Abuse at Columbia University. I gratefully agreed to help him launch the effort as a charter member of his first board.

10

In Good Company:
My Work in and with Medical Societies

I love what I do and don't apologize for committing so much of my life to my work. My family, fortunately, has been understanding, but I know it has often been very frustrating for Ruthie and Donney when I was forced to pass up a social event or a family outing to care for my patients.

On a typical weekday I go to bed between 8:30 and 9:00 in the evening in order to wake up by 4:00 a.m. and get to the hospital by 5:00 or 6:00 in the morning to begin rounds, hold office hours, tend to my paperwork, and perform two or three operations before noon. Barring emergencies or scheduled speeches and lectures out of town, my afternoons are usually devoted to meetings, conferences and calls to the various organizations with which I remain active. On Monday, my major teaching day, I moderate grand rounds with students and residents at Howard University Hospital in the morning and judge case presentations by junior-year medical students in the afternoon.

Why do I keep such a demanding schedule? Several years ago, a patient with a suspicious mammogram told me she had waited in anguish for weeks to get an appointment with me. I decided not to allow that to happen again and began holding office hours at 5:00 a.m. on Saturdays to make sure I was accessible to as many patients as possible. I usually see thirty to forty patients on Saturdays, primarily for brief follow-up visits after surgery, in order to reserve more time during the week for new-patient visits, which take more time. I also try to keep my Saturday schedule open to ensure that my patients can schedule appointments within a few days, rather than weeks, if this is necessary.

I realized early on that to drive my career as an academic surgeon I needed to participate in professional organizations that brought me in touch with my peers. Those groups sometimes posed tough challenges, but where there were barriers, I pressed forward with the determination my parents taught me—but without the bombast I displayed in that first local cancer society confrontation, of course.

My early forays into the world of professional medical societies actually grew out of disappointed ambition. Not long after joining the Howard faculty I was nominated to be a Markle Scholar, an honor awarded to promising surgeons who plan to devote themselves to academic careers. The award provides five years of funding for education and research costs and considerable prestige to go with it. But I was passed over for the award. Rather than pout or blame some hidden racism, however, I decided that to become both an expert teacher *and* a stellar clinical researcher, I would be active in local, national, and even international, health organizations and surgical and oncological societies. I would expand my network of contacts and increase my career opportunities. With determination and discipline, I set out to become one of the best surgical academicians ever—with or without a Markle award. By being passed over for this prize, I gained additional incentive to excel.

During my first year on Howard's faculty, 1962, I joined the surgical section of the National Medical Association (NMA), an organization founded by African-American physicians denied

131

membership in the American Medical Association (AMA), which until World War II was an all-white organization. It has been suggested by some that once black doctors were accepted into the AMA, there was no longer a reason to keep the NMA. But I side with those who argue that it will be a quite awhile still before black voices can be fully heard in a large national organization. I believe that we should preserve the NMA as a forum for our special concerns, especially that of looking out for the health care needs of underprivileged groups.

I later joined and became president of the Society of Black Academic Surgeons (SBAS), a group formed to encourage and nurture black surgeons. When I was a resident I knew the name of every black surgeon in the country who had been certified by the American Board of Surgery. I had also personally met many of them—there were only about 30. By the time the SBAS was founded nearly forty years later, our numbers had swelled to about 250. I was particularly proud that one of my successors as president of the group was Edward E. Cornwell III, a former student of mine and an honors graduate from Howard. Cornwell is currently a professor and chief of adult trauma at Johns Hopkins.

Founded as the James Ewing Society (in honor of Dr. Ewing, known as the "Father of Oncology") in 1940, the society changed its name to the Society of Surgical Oncology (SSO) in 1975. This organization, which I joined in 1964, is active in education, research, training, and liaison with other oncological organizations. SSO represents the largest group of cancer surgeons in the world—now with almost two thousand members.

The SSO was also the first national organization to name me as president, back in the days when we were still deciding just what surgical oncology was. The year was 1978, and the organization had just won allocation of a million-dollar grant from the National Cancer Institute for cancer research.

"I have seen the human condition in peril," I told my colleagues at my installation, "I have seen the stubborn persistence of hope when under ordinary circumstances there should be no hope. I have seen patients who seem to regard life itself as a constant opponent. I have seen an exhibition of faith that comes from those of strong moral fiber. I have seen the eyes of patients that seem to ask questions with 'the dignity of mute entreaty.' I have seen a demonstration of courage that defies description. And when I see these and more, it lets me know that as oncologists we must be more sensitive, more caring, and more compassionate to the patients committed to our care."

Nearly three decades later, I wouldn't take back a word.

In 1987 Dr. Robert Hutter, who was the president of the SSO, invited me to present the prestigious James Ewing lecture in London, where the society was meeting in conjunction with the British Association of Surgical Oncology and the British Society of Head and Neck Surgeons. Diana, princess of Wales, came to the awards banquet as a representative of the royal family. During dinner she told me of her good friend's father, who had just died of a particular form of cancer. She asked me what kind of research was being done in that area. Nine years later, during one of her visits to the United States, we met again at a dinner in the nation's capital to raise funds for the Nina Hyde Center for Breast Cancer Research. Ruthie and I were seated at her table, and Princess Diana mentioned the discussion she and I had all those years before. She asked me again about the progress we had made in her friend's area of concern in the intervening time. We also talked about her remarkably successful fund-raising efforts for breast cancer research.

Although she engaged in many charitable activities around the world, Princess Diana focused particularly on AIDS and breast cancer research. She once organized an auction of her gowns that raised millions of dollars for five cancer and AIDS charities in Britain and the United States, only a few months before her death in August 1997. Her activism and the high level of international cooperation between the SSO and British oncology groups reflect the breadth of the global network involved in attempting to make real progress in the fight against cancer.

Sometimes the causes in which I have become involved are less well known but equally deserving. For example, when I learned that South Africa had only about five hundred black doctors to serve that nation's majority black population of thirty-two million, I immediately agreed to join the board of Medical Education for South African Blacks, or MESAB, a foundation dedicated to educating black health care workers in that country. I continue to serve on that organization's medical advisory board. A joint U.S.–South African effort founded by Americans Joy and Herbert Kaiser, MESAB has dramatically increased the number of black physicians and other health care providers in South Africa in the last fifteen years, but the needs are still enormous as AIDS and other diseases continue to take a catastrophic toll on this long-disadvantaged population.

I've also been active for years with the Dana Foundation, a philanthropic organization founded by the late industrialist Charles A. Dana to support projects in neuroscience, immunology, and arts education. The foundation's former chairman, David Mahoney, invited me to join its board after the foundation established a panel to study the impact of heart disease, cancer, and stroke on the brain. In 2000 the foundation sent a specialist in each of those fields to speak to the World Economic Forum in Davos, Switzerland. That forum concentrates on political, economic, and social issues, but our session drew a standing-room-only crowd of several hundred. The panelists all agreed that, although it is difficult to prove, there does appear to be a connection between a person's attitude and his or her quality of life during and after life-threatening illness. It has not yet been demonstrated that people can will themselves to live longer, they claimed, but those with strong faith or a highly spiritual approach to life frequently do better during treatment and recovery than those who despair and surrender to their physical condition.

I was serving as master of ceremonies at a General Motors awards banquet for cancer research when I first met Lenore and Walter Annenberg. We hit it off instantly, and they invited Ruthie and me to join them at their Sunnylands estate in California to discuss our mutual interest in education. Annenberg had founded *TV Guide* magazine and built a media empire around it. He was thinking about ways he could use his fortune to help mankind. When we arrived, they showed us around their lovely home and their exquisite art collection, but what most impressed Ruthie and me was the Annenbergs' sincere interest in improving public education and their curiosity about the nation's historically black colleges and universities such as Howard. We talked about these schools' objectives, although we never spoke about money, and Walter listened intently as I described my commitment to Howard, its needs, and the needs of the other schools like it.

Ruthie and I were stunned—along with the rest of the country—when the Annenbergs announced soon after our visit that they were giving $50 million to the United Negro College Fund, a gift that far outstripped any other in the fund's history. I would like to think that our chat had some influence on their decision, but I guess I'll never know.

In 1963, during my second year on Howard's faculty, I went to the historic March on Washington led by Dr. Martin Luther King, Jr. Organizers of the march had asked Howard Med to provide medical teams for first aid stations to be set up around the Mall, and I was thrilled to volunteer and be of service in the way I knew best.

We were equipped to care for anyone who was injured or fell ill in the crush of the quarter-million demonstrators crowding the Mall and its adjoining broad avenues that memorable August day. Despite some predictions of violence, the march was blessedly peaceful and good-natured. The only activity we saw at our aid station were a few cases of heat stroke and dehydration.

Although I was serving behind the scenes, I felt very much a part of that incomparable scene. King's voice reverberated through the crowd and across the airwaves, elevating the spirits of people around the world: "We have also come to this hallowed spot to remind America of the fierce urgency of Now," he exhorted. "This is no time to engage in the luxury of cooling off or to take the tranquilizing drug of gradualism. Now is the time to make real the promises of democracy. Now is the time to rise from the dark and desolate valley of segregation to the sunlit path of racial justice. Now is the time to lift our nation from the quicksands of racial injustice to the solid rock of brotherhood. Now is the time to make justice a reality for all of God's children."

Like millions, I was inspired and encouraged by King's power and vision. Yet nearly twenty years later, I was painfully reminded how far my nation still had to go to reach the reality he foresaw.

It was 1982, and I already had been president of the American Cancer Society and the Society of Surgical Oncology. That year, two white colleagues from the Medical College of Virginia in Richmond, Dr. Shelton Horsley and Dr. Walter Lawrence, sponsored me for membership in the Southern Surgical Association. Horsley, Lawrence, and I all knew that my obtaining membership wouldn't be easy. "The Southern," as the organization is known in the profession, had a revered surgical tradition and a membership roster that—despite its name—came from all areas of the United States. But even in 1982, even not a single member was black.

I also had the support of Dr. Robert Coffey, a former president of the Southern and a close adviser, who told me at one of our frequent luncheons together that there were some members of the organization who probably wouldn't vote for my admission "even if I discovered a cure for cancer." He urged me not to be discouraged, however, and assured me, "You'll get in."

My nomination was rejected, nonetheless. Two years in a row! I finally asked the colleagues who had twice sponsored me to withdraw my name from the list of candidates. They were furious at what had happened and said so in a letter to the organization's executive committee. Lawrence even resigned from the Southern in protest but urged Horsley, his fellow sponsor, to stay and keep up the fight from inside the organization.

In 1985 Drs. James Hardy and Dean Warren, distinguished surgical academicians and former presidents of the Southern, resubmitted my name. The following year I was elected to membership along with my longtime friend and colleague, Dr. Claude Organ. Dr. Asa Yancey was the first black accepted into the Southern the prior year. I have enjoyed the social and scientific milieu of the Southern ever since. My good friend Dr. Lawrence rejoined in 1986, becoming first vice president in 2000 and an Honorary Fellow in 2004.

Congratulatory notes flowed in to me from the members of this group upon my acceptance, and one in particular touched me. That message came from Dr. Charles Watt, a surgeon from Thomasville, Georgia. Thomasville is a small city about fifty miles north of Quincy, Florida, my hometown. It is known as a bastion of northern wealth and southern tradition, as the center of a plantation economy for much of the nineteenth century, and later as a popular resort for wealthy Yankees who built grand "winter homes" and established their own society to which they escaped from frigid New York and New England. Watt not only celebrated my election but later invited me to stay at his home, deliver a named lecture, and visit the renowned Archbold Memorial Hospital, which I had heard about since childhood as our region's equivalent of the Mayo Clinic.

Several of those who wrote letters of congratulations praised my refusal to take my case public or make a racial issue out of those repeated rejections. I've often thought long and hard about that, and all I can say is that while I have enormous respect for Dr. King and wholeheartedly supported him and other freedom fighters who made the civil rights movement arguably the major force in our quest for social justice and equality, I've always believed that the greatest contribution I could make to those suffering injustice was to do my best and let my medical service set the example and prepare the way for others. I also remind myself of the debt I owe to men like Lawrence and Horsley, Hardy and Warren, who fought hard to open up the membership of otherwise racially exclusive organizations and give others the opportunities they enjoyed—based on merit and not artificial barriers.

The American Cancer Society is widely known, much less so than the other ACS in my life: the American College of Surgeons. The college is a scientific and educational association made up exclusively of surgeons. Founded in 1913, it is dedicated to promoting the ethical and competent practice of surgery combined with high quality care for the surgical patient. The college's educational programs are designed primarily to help surgeons render the best patient care possible. Even more than earning board certification in one's specialty, being admitted to fellowship in the college attests to a high level of training, professional competence, and ethical conduct.

In 1964, two years after being discharged from the Army and embarking on my career at Howard, I was awarded the privilege of adding the college's badge of honor, the letters FACS, after the M.D. tagged onto my name. The ACS is not a small, self-perpetuating club—there are 64,000 ACS fellows in the United States and 3,700 in other countries—but within my profession, membership in this group sets one apart.

I reached this highest level of surgical accreditation, I believe, partly due to my own initiative, my intensive study habits, my broad exposure to the fine points and rough edges of the profession and partly, to some degree, to my nearly lifelong love of the practice of medicine. I had also served on several ACS committees involved with educational, legislative, and socioeconomic issues. Along the way, I received immeasurable help from friends and colleagues and tried to use my influence as a college insider to open the doors for others.

In 1972 the late Dr. Earl Belle Smith of Pittsburgh and I went to visit the college's director as representatives of the surgical section of the National Medical Association. We wanted to propose that our section be allowed to become more involved in ACS programs and committees. The director at that time, C. Rollins "Rollo" Hanlon, listened attentively and later took our concerns to his board, which later significantly enhanced the organization's outreach efforts.

Several years later, in 1983, I was elected secretary of the college, a position I held for nine years. I soon became known to most members of the group, but in June 1986 a single incident somehow changed the way my colleagues looked at me. They saw something in me I didn't expect—and can't really explain.

Oliver "Ollie" Beahrs, a senior surgeon at the Mayo Clinic and chairman of the college's board of regents, invited me to be the closing speaker at a testimonial dinner for Rollo Hanlon. Everyone had enjoyed a delicious dinner and plenty of wine. There had been more than enough excellent tributes to a most deserving guest of honor, and when I finally got up to speak shortly before midnight, my audience was benumbed. I could see bobbing heads, drooping eyelids, and people looking around for the exits. What a challenge!

I had long admired Rollo's fierce commitment to patients and his unwavering support for surgeons, and I had thought a lot about what I wanted to say. As was my custom, however, I did not write a speech, and I don't remember exactly what I said. But I must have touched many a responsive chord. When I finished, the attendees jumped to their feet to give me a standing ovation!

Richard Field, a regent from Centreville, Mississippi, told me afterward that many people felt sorry for me when I got up to the lectern to speak because no one was in the mood for another talk. But, he said, "We'll never forget that moment."

"We may not remember anything you said, but we'll never forget the way you said it," he stated good-naturedly. "You reached a new level."

Letters flowed in from friends and colleagues for weeks afterward with comments like, "Yours was one of the very finest speeches I have ever heard in all my born days"; "Splendid tribute . . . it brought tears to some eyes"; "The high spot of the evening . . . you said it better than anyone else could have"; and "Best I've ever heard."

Upon reflection, I look back on that talk as an indication of the additional something I had to offer. I believe, first of all, that I was recognized by my colleagues as one of the leaders in my field of specialization—surgical oncology. Certainly, speaking well—saying things in a way that people will remember them and the occasion—is vital to being a leader of large groups that organize themselves around big meetings and conferences. That's one reason why I've always tried to speak from the heart to let audiences know that my feelings are genuine. I've also been a strong believer in the expression, "You can disagree with someone without being disagreeable." I have never played the role of sycophant for anyone, but no matter what the dispute may be, I try never to express any rancor or rudeness. As a result, I have won respect from people with whom I've had quite fundamental disagreements because I always sought to work with them, even while openly acknowledging our differences.

For these reasons, I believe, people and organizations have come to understand that when I agree to take on a particular assignment or position, they can count on me to commit myself wholeheartedly to the endeavor and give my absolute best.

Some nine years after that late-night speech in Chicago, I attained what I still regard as the zenith of my professional achievements: On October 26, 1995, I was installed as president of the American College of Surgeons, an honor that exceeded my wildest dreams and once again marked me as the first black leader of an organization known throughout the world for its pursuit of excellence.

If only my mother and father could have seen me that night! In accepting my new responsibilities in my presidential address to the group in New Orleans—with my wife, son, sister, sister-in-law and her surgeon husband, many friends, and colleagues looking on—I pledged to uphold the highest standards of the ACS but noted that the occasion symbolized much more to me than that. "It also serves as a catalyst," I said, "that I hope will lead to increased diversity in college activities that can only add to our strength, commitment, and dedication."

"It is time," I added, "for a reaffirmation of fealty to the principles we hold dear and to be ever mindful of the creed emblazoned on the college seal: *Omnibus per artem—fidemque prodesse*—"To serve all, with skill and fidelity."

During my term the ACS made progress toward my goals of greater diversity and outreach by engaging its board of governors in in-depth discusions that would later lead to a formal statement from the organization's board of regents. It was not until 2000, however, that—thanks to the hard work of Drs. Clive Callender, Claude Organ, and William Matory (all fellows of the college and longtime colleagues in the surgical section of the National Medical Association), among many others—the college publicly committed itself to promoting the "pluralism and equal opportunity which recognizes and respects the diversity of its members in order to maintain the highest standards of leadership in the profession."

11

A War with Many Fronts:
Working for the Cure

The two most common cancers that I encountered in my practice when I returned to Howard's medical faculty after my Army tour of duty were breast and colorectal cancer. Often patients came to me in the advanced stages of the disease. Given the training I received at Memorial Sloan-Kettering, I decided to focus on these cancers for my clinical research studies.

The American Cancer Society asked me to chair a task force on cancers of the colon and rectum in 1973, and I hastily accepted, largely because my research and practice already indicated the increased vulnerability of African-Americans to these cancers, although I had not yet co-authored the landmark paper documenting it with my colleagues. I had, however, been involved in colorectal cancer projects with physicians from two of the nation's great cancer centers: M. D. Anderson in Houston and Sloan-Kettering in New York.

Seeing black patients with advanced stages of the disease in the numbers I did made me want to concentrate that much more on finding ways to diagnose them earlier. If detected before it spreads, colorectal cancer is today 90 percent curable, yet it is the second most deadly form of the disease, lung cancer being the leading killer. What makes those numbers most frustrating is that they mean we can save all but about 15,000 of the 57,000 people who will die from cancer of the colon or rectum this year—if only we catch their disease in time. It is no exaggeration to say the vast majority of those who die could be leading normal, cancer-free lives.

It is a great tragedy that most people don't know about or, more likely, just don't feel comfortable with the relatively simple screening procedures that can enable a doctor to catch the disease early, before it becomes a painful, heartbreaking, uncontrollable monster. By the time physicians diagnose the disease, two out of three cases already have progressed beyond the point where they face that ninety-percent cure rate cut-off, and they must begin struggling against the odds.

Much the same is true for breast cancer. The figures, screening, and treatment are somewhat different, but the key is the same: the sooner we can spot the disease, the better the patient's odds of long-term survival. Great progress has been made in recent years, thanks largely to breakthroughs in technology, but getting people in to be tested is still a challenge.

In my experience there are only two things that can force a reluctant patient to go to the doctor: pain and blood. If the pain is severe or persistent or the bleeding doesn't stop, people eventually seek help. The sad part is that, with breast cancer, there is rarely any pain or bleeding in the early stages. The dreadful pain associated with this disease generally comes at the end of its cycle, when the cancer has spread and little can be done to check its course.

On the other hand, bleeding is the most common symptom of colorectal cancer, but it often appears insignificant and occurs intermittently, as does the pain, which usually feels like stomach cramps. When the symptoms subside, however, the patient naturally assumes (or hopes) the problem has gone away and forgets about it.

The remarkable imaging technologies developed and improved upon since I first entered the medical profession make it possible today to see cancerous or even precancerous tumors long before they cause pain or bleeding and start to spread to other critical parts of the body. If we detect cancers early, we can take them out or kill them with drugs or radiation. Women who are taught to examine their own breasts for lumps may find tumors in an early stage, but a regular mammogram is the best way to pick up the first signs of disease. Most people who pay any attention at all to health stories on television or in other media know about early detection, but they often fail to apply it to their own lives. Also, health care in this country is expensive and often inconvenient—thus, it is almost always easier to put off than not.

Colon cancer's early detection rates are even worse than those for breast cancer. Long before the patient is aware of any symptoms—sometimes several years before—rogue cells start to grow deep in the recesses of the intestinal tract. They usually begin as tiny, benign polyps—bumps—on the inside wall of the colon. Eventually, if the polyps are left to grow, they may become malignant. Some symptoms will show up at this stage, usually a bit of rectal bleeding or blood in the stool, a change in bowel habits, chronic diarrhea or constipation, or persistent abdominal cramps. Even then, most people try to ignore the problem because they just aren't comfortable talking about their bowels or bowel habits with other people, even doctors.

Colon cancer strikes both men and women in about equal numbers, although women usually think of it as a "men's disease" and don't get tested for it as much as they should. One simple test, not as effective as more high-tech procedures, involves simply smearing a bit of stool on a piece of cardboard made for the purpose and mailing it to a lab. Lots of physicians hand out these test cards at the end of every physical exam they gie to their patients over age forty, but the return rate is disappointing. Patients just "forget" or simply throw the cards away.

In the 1970s, a device was developed that dramatically increased our ability to identify polyps and tumors in the colon and remove them before they caused trouble. The procedure is called a colonoscopy, and *every person over age fifty*—even younger if they have a family history of the disease—should have one every five to ten years. A colonoscopy is not particularly pleasant, but it is rarely onerous or dangerous, and it is one of the great lifesavers of modern medical science.

Here is the procedure:

The day before the colonoscopy exam, the patient begins taking a salty-tasting liquid or pills on a prescribed schedule to clean out the colon. We've tried to make this laxative taste less awful, but I recommend chasing it down with ginger ale to make it more palatable. Some people make a fuss about this, but it's really not that bad. It does, however, cause the patient to go to the bathroom more frequently, and it's important to keep taking the laxative on schedule to get the job done. This is because the scope used to examine the inside of the colon is a tiny video camera, and it must have a clear view of the colon wall in order for the doctor to spot any abnormalities.

Most people don't like the idea of having an instrument inserted into their rectum. They think it violates their privacy and dignity and might embarrass them. My advice to them is: Look, we're trying to save your life here, and a few minutes of discomfort are well worth it. Consider the alternatives!

The instrument used by the examiner, usually a gastroenterologist or colorectal surgeon who specializes in diseases of the digestive system, is a long, narrow, flexible tube with a tiny light and a surgical tool on the end. The latter is used to snip off polyps or take tissue samples for analysis in the lab. The patient lies on one side and is given a sedative to help him or her feel more relaxed and minimize the discomfort. Then the tube is inserted and carefully pushed up through the colon, twisting and turning to follow the natural curves of the lower intestine. The procedure takes about thirty or forty minutes, after which the patient is able to go home and resume normal activities.

That's it!

In most cases, if a polyp is discovered it can be removed on the spot without any pain or lengthy recovery time. If a cancerous lesion is found, surgery must be performed to remove the tumor and surrounding tissue, but that tremendously increases the chances of long-term survival. It used to be fairly common in such cases, perhaps 20 percent of the time, for physicians to perform a colostomy, leading the colon out to the abdominal wall and adding a bag to collect waste. The prospect of living with a colostomy bag was dreadful for many cancer patients because it was messy and forced them to change their lifestyle to accommodate it. Earlier diagnosis and changes in surgical techniques have enabled doctors to restore patients' normal bowel function after surgery in the vast majority of cases. We rarely have to attach colostomy bags anymore.

Many Americans remember that President Ronald Reagan underwent surgery for colon cancer that was discovered during a colonoscopy in 1985. In one of my first network television appearances I explained the procedure and the details of the president's treatment on the "CBS Evening News" with Dan Rather and later with Bob Schieffer. Reagan, of course, lived for many years with no recurrence of that cancer and led a remarkably active life until brought down by an unrelated illness: Alzheimer's disease.

Among the many calls I received after that news program, one from a favorite patient of mine, an inspiring octogenarian and a cancer survivor known for her infectious good humor, was the most rewarding. She called to say how proud she was to see a black professional on national television speaking authoritatively about a cancer operation "on no less than the president of the United States."

"Oh, Dr. Leffall," she said, "I'm so happy! I never thought I'd live to see the day when I'd see a black doctor do what you did!"

Reagan's experience, which received wide publicity because cancer had struck a sitting president in the midst of the Cold War, certainly contributed to public awareness and understanding of colon cancer and the importance of routine screening. No one, however, deserves more credit for focusing attention on the disease and its prevention than Katie Couric.

Ms. Couric, the popular cohost of NBC's "Today Show," lost her husband, Jay Monahan, to colon cancer when he was only forty-two. She resolved afterward to turn her personal tragedy into an opportunity to educate her audience of more than six million viewers—and millions more beyond the show—about the prevention, diagnosis, treatment and lethal nature of the disease that killed her husband. In September 1998 she recruited me as the surgical consultant for a weeklong series on her show called "Confronting Colon Cancer." NBC sent its cameras into the operating room while I was performing colon surgery. The cameras focused on the colon I removed with its cancerous tumor and polyps clearly visible.

Two years later, in an award-winning, five-part follow-up, Ms. Couric broadcast a videotape of her own first colonoscopy— a television breakthrough that showed her audience that the oft-dreaded procedure isn't as bad as the mind makes it out to be. "The prep is really worse than the procedure," she pronounced, and millions of Americans must have breathed a sigh of relief.

A study by University of Michigan and University of Iowa researchers found that the number of colonoscopies performed in the United States jumped more than twenty percent in the weeks after Ms. Couric's colonoscopy was shown on television. They dubbed it the "Couric Effect."

The "Today Show" televised another five-part series on colon cancer in the spring of 2004 in conjunction with Ms. Couric's opening of the Jay Monahan Center in New York. That center is truly a model for facilities that offer coordinated care and public education on gastrointestinal disorders.

We physicians are now much better about advising our patients to have colonoscopies than before, but we must continue to emphasize that many previously completely asymptomatic people have had screenings at age fifty or so and found tumors. The recent development of an imaging technology called "virtual colonoscopy" enables trained radiologists to see the inside of the colon wall without having to insert a scope into the rectum. I am hopeful that perfection of this technique will encourage more people to overcome their reluctance to get this all-important screening.

Celebrities often get people interested in specific diseases, either because their own cases play out in the public eye or because they devote their time and influence to raising awareness about the causes they care most about. This was especially true in the fight against breast cancer. Partly because Americans have long had a fascination with the female breast as a sex object, cancer of the breast was long seen as a shameful condition and often kept secret. Disfiguring surgery was to be avoided at all cost. In 1974, First Lady Betty Ford discovered only shortly after moving into the White House that she had breast cancer, and three weeks later Happy Rockefeller, wife of vice presidential nominee Nelson Rockefeller, learned she did, too. Both women courageously acknowledged their illness and the details of the surgery that saved their lives.

Soraya, the talented singer and songwriter who is also a breast cancer survivor, has been especially active in the Hispanic Latina community promoting breast cancer awareness and education. Child-movie-star-turned-diplomat Shirley Temple Black also took charge of her case and helped change the custom of letting doctors decide, while the patient is still under anesthesia, whether to remove a cancerous breast. "The doctor can make the incision; I'll make the decision," Ms. Black famously announced after a growth was found in her breast in 1972. She then chose a simple, rather than a radical, mastectomy and aggressive chemotherapy to treat her cancer. She has lived cancer-free for more than thirty years since.

Women in the early 1970s rarely made such critical decisions for themselves, but in the years since, it has become standard practice for women to discuss their options with their doctors before consenting to surgery, which today frequently involves only removal of the lump and the surrounding tissue rather than the whole breast.

The very public ordeals of such prominent women encouraged millions of others to learn to examine themselves for lumps and become aware of the signs of cancer. As the life-saving potential of mammography became clear, women increasingly have been encouraged to get annual imaging examinations earlier and earlier in their adult lives.

In 2002, former Senator Edward Brooke of Massachusetts called to tell me that he had been diagnosed with breast cancer, a condition that is rare in men but does occur from time to time, and it can be deadly when it does. Brooke asked me if he should "go public" and I encouraged him to do so to call attention to the need for men to be vigilant as well as women. The year after completing his treatment, he disclosed his experience and health status in an interview with the *New York Times*. At my request he also addressed a conference of the Susan G. Komen Breast Cancer Foundation. Brooke received overwhelming support from around the country and abroad and was gratified that he had sacrificed his privacy for the benefit of others.

Susan G. Komen, whose name is more closely associated with breast cancer awareness today than any other, was never a celebrity. "Suzy" Komen—as she was known to family and friends—was a Peoria, Illinois, housewife who was diagnosed with breast cancer in her thirties and fought the disease through nine operations, radiation treatment, and three courses of chemotherapy. In 1980 she lost her painful but determined three-year struggle. Two years later, her younger sister, Nancy Brinker, founded the Susan G. Komen Breast Cancer Foundation to carry out her sister's wish to help others battling the disease. The foundation's "Race for the Cure" draws millions of participants in cities across the country to raise money for breast cancer research and to call attention to the need for early screening and effective treatment.

With my interest in breast cancer, and having served on the Komen Foundation's board for several years, I was elected its chairman in 2002. Since its founding in 1982 the Komen Foundation has raised more than $740 million for the fight against breast cancer. It also reaches far beyond the obvious targets for prevention and screening activities to reach out to the medically underserved and minorities—black, Hispanic, Asian, and Native Americans; Pacific Islanders; Alaskan Natives; and any others we can identify. Senator Ed Brooke works with us to increase men's awareness of their vulnerability to breast cancer.

Because African-American women have a disproportionately high death rate from breast cancer, I also work with Zora Kramer Brown, a fourth-generation breast cancer survivor and founder of the Breast Cancer Resource Committee, and Karen Jackson of Sisters Network. Both women have effectively focused attention on the special needs of African-American women, encouraging them to come in for mammograms and conduct routine self-exams.

Many families have some member who has been affected by cancer, and mine is no exception. While I was serving as national president of the American Cancer Society, my father-in-law developed lung cancer that could be treated only with radiation and chemotherapy. On our numerous visits to see him in Richmond, Ruthie and I observed firsthand the effects of the energy-draining therapy he was receiving. Throughout his illness, however, he maintained a positive attitude and exhibited no self-pity. His wife was a true stalwart and excellent caregiver who provided great moral and physical support. After several months he succumbed to his disease. This personal experience emphasized something that I already knew: cancer indeed affects the entire family.

My mother used to visit me and my family in Washington each summer. She loved good food, and I always made it a point to take her to the Jockey Club in the old Fairfax Hotel for a mother-son lunch. She always ordered the Dover Sole. We would invariably talk about my father and recall stories of my growing up in Quincy.

In the summer of 1993, during our annual outing at the Jockey Club, I noticed that Mother wasn't eating her favorite dish and asked if anything was wrong. She said she hadn't had much of an appetite the last two or three months and had a bit of an upset stomach. My first thought, of course, was cancer. Knowing Mother was eighty-four years old and hearing her talk about her chronic indigestion, I realized instantly that we needed more information.

I took her to Howard University Hospital the next day, where blood tests and a colonoscopy strongly indicated she had an advanced malignancy. There was no sign of a visible tumor, but the abnormal stiffening of her colon suggested that malignant cells were infiltrating the wall of the colon. I suspected that her disease was ovarian cancer, and I immediately picked Dr. Russell Hill, a gynecological cancer surgeon at Howard, to operate on Mother to determine what was causing the problem and whether anything could be done to fix it. I asked another young surgeon whom I had trained, Dr. Wayne B. Tuckson,[3] a colorectal specialist, to assist Dr. Hill.

Mother asked me before the surgery if her problems could be cancer-related, and although I knew the evidence was very

---

[3] Tuckson later established the LaSalle D. Leffall Jr. Surgical Society at Howard's medical school.

strong, I said only that it could be, but, not necessarily so. I had to leave her some room for hope, just as I would for any patient.

When my colleagues operated, they found cancer throughout my mother's abdominal cavity. What had begun as an ovarian tumor had spread, and malignant nodules studded her abdominal lining. I was devastated. There I was—a prominent cancer surgeon, a leading member of my profession, a recipient of the finest training in the world—and I couldn't save my own mother!

I waited until the next day to give Mother a chance to clear away the fog of anesthesia and post-op pain medication, then I walked into her hospital room determined not to let my expression give away what I knew. She took one look at my face, however, and immediately said, "It was cancer, wasn't it?"

It was one of the most heart-piercing statements I have ever heard.

I nodded mechanically, and she asked if anything could be done. "We'll see," I said, "But there won't be any more surgical treatment. Radiation would not be effective, but I will talk to my colleagues about whether any drugs might help."

Because of her age and the extensive surgery she had just undergone, Mother was in an intensive care unit directed by two young surgeons I had helped train, Drs. Suryanarayana Siram and Haile Mezghebe. They later came to talk with me as a team and asked me for guidance about what to do if my mother were to stop breathing and needed life support. I simply said, "No heroic measures."

That's not an easy thing to say, ever, and not just because she was my mother. But I felt very deeply then—and still feel just as strongly—that when you know what the outcome will be, when you know a person's cancer is in such an advanced stage that nothing can be done, adding a few days or weeks to their suffering is not heroic.

If there had been the slightest possibility that Mother would have gotten better and been released from the hospital to enjoy some time with her family, my decision would have been different. But I knew that was not an option. I knew, given the advanced stage of her disease, she might have been kept alive for an additional month or two, but it would not have been a life as she had known it or a life she would have wanted to live.

As a physician who has dealt with patients in the final stages of life for more than a half-century, I know it is not just that patients live but *how* they live that's important. The quality of a patient's life is critical. I felt comfortable making that decision for my own mother, but it was still not an easy thing to say: "If my mother stops breathing, do not resuscitate."

Blessedly, within three weeks of her surgery, Mother's vital organs began to shut down. She developed major lung and kidney problems and failed very fast. The doctors came to me again to ask if I was firm in my decision. I said I was, and they told me she could stop breathing at any time.

I went to her room and sat silently beside her, and I was there when she took her last breath. I saw my mother die.

I stayed with Mother for a few moments afterward, said a silent prayer for her, and went back to my office to be alone. After a few minutes, I picked up the phone and called my sister Dolores, then my wife and son. We flew Mother's body back to Quincy, where she had lived since 1932, and buried her next to her husband—my father—just as she had asked.

12

Only One Continent to Go!:
Medical Journeys and Discoveries in Foreign Lands

In my travels for the American Cancer Society, I advocated for more active cancer screening programs, early diagnosis, and treatment. As my reputation grew I was invited to lecture around the world on the latest techniques for and principles of treating cancers of the breast and colon. I often spoke about other areas in which I had expertise such as cancers of the head and neck.

My first trip to speak abroad was to Germany, where I had done my military service. One of my German colleagues, Dr. Andreas Schnur, who had helped Ruthie and me get settled overseas and coached me in German, invited me back in 1965 to address the Bavarian Surgical Congress in Erlangen. It is customary at these lectures to review the state of the art of the subject at hand and to pass along any particular techniques one believes might be helpful to other surgeons. Dr. Schnur suggested I talk about cancers of the head and neck, knowing that I was interested in that area, and he encouraged me to give my lecture in German.

My talk was thus entitled, "Diagnose und Behandlung von Speicheldruesen Tumoren," or "Diagnosis and Treatment of Salivary Gland Tumors." I wrote it in English, then sent it to Dr. Schnur, who translated it for me. I practiced the speech many times before I left Washington. However, to make sure I could deliver it properly, I stopped in Munich on my way to Erlangen, a Bavarian university town just north of Nuremberg, and went over it with Dr. Schnur to brush up on the language. He also asked me several hypothetical questions that he thought were likely to come up at the lecture, and I responded to those in German as well, improving my answers with his coaching.

When I later delivered the talk, which was about a half-hour long, my German colleagues were most receptive and thankfully polite during the question-and-answer session that followed. They spoke clearly, posed their queries slowly, and generously did not try to stump me with complicated questions that would outdistance my ability to respond in German.

Without getting as technical here as I had to in speaking to my German fellow surgeons, the thrust of my talk was on maintaining what I call a "high index of suspicion" when examining patients for possible cancers of the parotid gland, the gland that swells when a person gets mumps, or of another salivary gland called the submandibular beneath the lower jaw. If the symptoms of these cancers, such as lumps, soreness, or swelling in the mouth don't go away after a couple of weeks, I noted, physicians have reason for concern and should prescribe careful follow-up. When operating on the parotid gland, I explained the importance of identifying the facial nerve that exits from the skull next to the gland and of being careful not to injure it. If that nerve is damaged, the patient may survive the cancer but be forced to live with a twisted face. Surgeons who perform that operation know the importance of that nerve, but sometimes it can be difficult to find. I tried to give my audience some tips for doing so, and most of the questions after my talk centered on that issue.

I was both proud of myself and gratified that I was able to respond in German, and the audience heartily applauded my effort, but that was nothing compared to what happened thirty-two years later when I returned to Germany to accept an honorary fellowship in the German Surgical Society.

My language skills had become somewhat rusty over three decades hence, but I was determined to give my acceptance speech in German when Ruthie and I returned to Munich for the society's annual meeting. Dr. Schnur was there, as were several other German surgeons whom I had come to know over the years. In my remarks, I mentioned that while serving in the Army I had spent a day with the great professor of surgery, Dr. Rudolf Zenker. (Of course, I didn't mention that I had also dared ask Zenker a question during surgery and been cut off by one of his assistants.)

After my talk, I returned to my front-row seat next to Ruthie, and as the proceedings resumed an elderly woman came down the aisle from the back of the auditorium. She walked directly up to my seat. I had no idea who she was.

"Ich bin Frau Zenker," she said, tears streaming down her cheeks, "die Witwe von Herrn Professor Zenker."

It was Dr. Zenker's widow, and she was overjoyed at my warm comments about her late husband. The audience of about 1,500 burst into applause and stopped the program for several minutes as I spoke with Frau Zenker at the front of the big hall.

Ruthie told me afterward how surprised she was that I had no idea who the woman was who was rushing toward us. "Who else could it have been?" she asked, as if it were obvious to everyone in the room except me. Perhaps it was.

Another surgeon from an even earlier stage in my career led to my first trip to Africa. I was, of course, eager to visit the continent of my ancestors and see for myself the state of health care in that part of the world. A friend, Latunde Odeku of Nigeria, had been a medical student at Howard two years behind me.

After Odeku completed his training in neurosurgery at the University of Michigan, he returned home to teach and practice at the University of Ibadan, site of his country's most prestigious medical school. Odeku was extremely bright and could have worked in almost any medical center in the world that he chose, but he was determined to go back to help upgrade the level of care in his home country. He became the first black neurosurgeon on the continent of Africa. He and I kept in touch over the years, and Ruthie and I used to see him when he would stop at Howard on his way to surgical conferences in the United States. In 1972 Dr. Odeku invited me to come to Ibadan as an external examiner to evaluate medical students and critique teaching and surgical practices at his university. I jumped at the chance to visit Nigeria, a country of over a hundred million people, the most populous nation in Africa.

The university had a huge hospital with more than a thouand beds. I was delighted to find high standards of practice and modern equipment, most of it from the United Kingdom, where the majority of Ibadan's medical students get their advanced training. The medical center lacked some of the very latest technology, such as a linear accelerator used to kill cancer with radiation, but I was generally impressed by the high level of the equipment and the quality of care. What set this hospital apart from what I was used to seeing was the advanced state of diseases treated there. During my stay I worked as a visiting professor as well as an examiner. I also lectured on breast cancer, made rounds with hospital students and staff, and operated on patients alongside my Nigerian colleagues.

I saw no colon cancer because that particular disease is relatively uncommon in Africa, but I was regularly confronted with very advanced breast cancers, particularly among women from rural areas surrounding Ibadan. I saw giant-size hernias and thyroids in patients who clearly never came to a clinic until their disease was far beyond what doctors normally see in the United States.

157

While I was in Ibadan, a patient was brought in from a village outside the city. She had an ulcerating tumor involving half or three-quarters of one breast that was oozing blood and emitting an odor so foul that it repulsed and nauseated her. She thought it was just a bad infection. When I explained to her what cancer was, she said she didn't believe she had that, but she begged me to do something about the smell that made her own children and family shy away from her.

Cancer tumors feed on the body's blood, and the woman's massive, untreated malignancy had outgrown its blood supply and become an open sore. I removed the breast and all the cancerous tissue I could. A plastic surgeon was able to cover the defect to enable the wound to heal. She and her family were most grateful, and the woman went home feeling better and free of the sickening odor. I had no illusions that we had cured her—the disease was far too advanced to expect that—but we had provided palliative care and had certainly improved the quality of her life.

My Nigerian colleagues kept me informed about the woman after I left, and a year later her cancer had not returned. After that she was, in medical terms, "lost to follow-up," meaning she didn't return to see doctors, and I received no more reports. I'm certain, however, that we gave her at least a year of a much better life than she could have led without our help.

I stayed in Ibadan for a couple of weeks, living in faculty quarters on campus and visiting the homes of medical professors for dinner or going out with them to nearby restaurants. When I wasn't conducting my formal evaluation or working at the hospital, my hosts drove me into the countryside to visit some of the outlying clinics. There they saw patients whose conditions were too advanced to be treated by the local health care workers. People in these villages lived in huts, and their clinics were small wooden buildings of similar construction. I saw a number of cancer cases on those trips, particularly cancer of the breast, one of the most common malignancies in that region. By the time I saw them, however, their disease had progressed quite far because many of them relied first on what we Westerners call nontraditional methods of care such as potions and prayer. They usually sought modern medical help only after other efforts had failed.

Dr. Odeku was an excellent surgeon, totally committed to his homeland, and an accomplished poet as well. A collection of his poetry, entitled *Twilight Out of the Night*, was published in 1964. Ruthie and I treasure the copy he signed for us during my visit in 1972. I have quoted one of his poems for years hence in speeches I delivered to students because I think it encourages them to give of themselves to others. It is called "Learning to Expect":

> I have learnt to expect
> From life but just a little;
> From the words of men,
> Only that which is due;
> And their promises,
> Only what they can do.
>
> I have learnt to expect
> From the sun not a miracle,
> But the share that sweat can bring
> For its worth.
>
> I have learnt to expect
> That tomorrow will forget
> What you and I exalt today;
> Not to spite our being,
> Only to know
> That in the limits of the universe
> Ours is but a little place;
> High perhaps in the sight of God,
> But, in the ultimate scheme of things to come,
> A speck of dust.

Unfortunately, my visit to Ibadan was the last time I saw Dr. Odeku. He died of heart disease in 1974 while still a comparatively young man. I was pleased to learn afterward that the university named its medical library in his honor.

In later trips to Africa I visited Abidjan, capital of the Ivory Coast, where I represented the American College of Surgeons at the twenty-fifth anniversary celebration of the West African College of Surgeons. I spoke there on managing late carcinoma of the breast, a pervasive problem throughout the continent, as I had seen in Ibadan more than a decade before. I also toured Cape Town, South Africa, where I made rounds at Groote Schuur Hospital, the medical center where Dr. Christiaan Barnard performed the first human heart transplant in 1967.

During American Cancer Society trips to South America—including Bolivia, Chile, Peru, and Argentina—I joined delegations that emphasized screening and early detection, especially of breast and cervical cancer. These visits were of great value to our hosts because their nations were reporting increasing numbers of patients with advanced stages of cancer. My travels to the northern reaches of the American continent have taken me to Montreal, Canada, where I delivered the Charles Drew Lecture at McGill University. I have also given the annual Kergin lecture at the University of Toronto.

Sometimes my foreign travel was as much a learning experience for me as it was for the hosts who invited me to lecture and make rounds. Primary liver cancer—that is, tumors that originate in the liver as opposed to those that spread to that vital organ—is a particular problem in Asia. In Hong Kong and Singapore, I observed new techniques for resection of the liver, a surgical procedure that is much more common in Asia because those regions see so much primary liver cancer.

A trip to Australia included a visit to the Sydney Cancer Center. There, I was informed about the most recent advances in screening, diagnosis, and treatment of malignant melanoma—

one of the most common cancers seen in that region. I was also invited by my friend Penne Peacock to speak to an enthusiastic group of cancer center supporters at the famous Sydney Opera House.

I visited Iran before the revolution that overthrew the shah and led to the seizure of American hostages in the U.S. Embassy for 444 days. I took Ruthie, Donney, and his prep school classmate Peter Folger to Shiraz, where I was a visiting professor at Pahlavi University medical school for six weeks. I was there primarily to lecture on oncology at one of the two medical schools in non-English-speaking countries where instruction was given in English. (The other was at the American University in Beirut, Lebanon.) It was 1977, and Shah Mohammad Reza Pahlavi was still viewed in the United States as a visionary leader trying to modernize his oil-rich nation by borrowing ideas and talent from the West and establishing alliances with strategic partners like the United States. From Tehran's pristine, efficient airport to the swank high-rise apartments in the city's commercial districts, from its beautifully landscaped parks and public areas to its modern highways and power plants, Iran seemed to represent enlightened wealth and progress built on ancient Persian traditions and two-and-a-half centuries of monarchy. How little did we know!

I nonetheless enjoyed the opportunity to teach Iranian medical students and residents in their modern hospital. I made rounds with them, and I scrubbed and went to the operating room with residents as they operated on patients with breast cancer or intestinal problems. I also learned to treat the hydatid cysts that are caused by a parasite endemic in Middle Eastern livestock. The typical Iranian diet relies heavily on the meat of sheep and goats, which carry the parasite and pass it along to humans. The disease, then almost unknown in the United States, has become more common with increased trade and immigration, although it is still rare in most parts of our country. If not diagnosed and treated, these cysts can rupture and cause patient death.

While I was teaching, Ruthie, Donney, and Peter traveled around the country learning about Iran and its history. Donney especially remembers visiting the ancient ceremonial capital of Persepolis. He was studying American poets in school, and he was impressed that the Iranian people revered their poets, erecting statues to honor Saadi, a thirteenth-century poet known for his maxims; Hafez, a fourteenth-century writer; and Ferdowsi, whose epic in rhyme chronicled the growth of civilization before the Arab conquest in the seventh century.

I wish I had listened more carefully when the Iranian medical students who gave me a tour of Shiraz told me that the shah was out of touch with his people and was using the military and secret police to brutally suppress his opposition. Two years later, when the shah was overthrown by fundamentalist Islamic revolutionaries, I was sorry I had dismissed the students' warnings as the complaints of ill-informed youth. It was easy to be blinded by the lush lifestyle of my hosts and the reassuring talk of Ardeshir Zahedi, the shah's friendly, popular and skillful ambassador to the United States.

I suspect it was Zahedi who helped arrange a surprise capstone to my trip: two seats in the Royal Box at Wimbledon for the final match between Sweden's Bjorn Borg and American Jimmy Connors in a thrilling tennis classic that happened to coincide with our trip home from Iran through London. I remember Donney and I ate the traditional strawberries and Devonshire cream at intermission during the centennial celebration of the famed British tournament, then returned to our seats to watch Donney's favorite, Borg, defeat my favorite, Connors, in a heartstopping six games to four to take the fifth and final set of the championship match.

Few of my trips have had such a spectacular finish.

The British especially know how to enjoy pageantry protocol, as I found out in 2004 as I stood listening to the herald trumpeters announce the opening of the Royal College of Surgeons of Eng-

land. I then marched behind a mace-bearing marshal in my flow-
ing blue-and-scarlet robes and matching blue velvet cap to accept an honorary fellowship in that British society founded in
1540. Sir Peter Morris, president of the college and former chief
of surgery at Oxford University, presented me with my parch-
ment after reading a generous citation noting my "most profound
and lasting contribution" as an educator and leader of my
profession.

I should confess that not all the trappings were new to me.
For nine years, as secretary of the American College of Surgeons,
I carried a similar mace, an ornate ceremonial staff that had been
presented to the organization in 1920 by a committee of British
surgeons who had worked side by side with their American
counterparts during World War I. Sir Berkeley Moynihan, perhaps his country's best-known abdominal surgeon and a professor of surgery at Leeds University, offered that mace as "a
symbol of our union in the harsh days of trial" with the hope
that the surgeons of both lands "shall be joined in brotherhood
forever in the service of mankind."

I have continued to travel for both ACS's and for various
other organizations that have sought my help over the years.
When Nancy Brinker, founder of the Susan G. Komen Breast
Cancer Foundation, was United States ambassador to Hungary,
for example, she invited me, as the foundation's chairman, to
Budapest to promote early breast cancer detection among lay
and professional groups there. When I visited the Hungarian Oncology Institute in 2003, much attention was still focused on advanced stages of the disease. I tried to emphasize both the
importance of teaching women self-examination techniques and
the importance of mammography. Nancy promoted early detection in Hungary, as she has elsewhere, even then; and there already is evidence that the number of such programs is growing
in that nation. She hopes to extend them to more Eastern European countries as part of the Komen Foundation's efforts.

I also visited Rome in 2004 after the Komen Foundation

launched an Italian version of its hugely popular Race for the Cure, led by the Italian surgeon Riccardo Masetti. The foundation now sponsors a similar race in Frankfurt, Germany.

Foreign travel has shown me that the world's people have many common problems that my cancer specialist colleagues and I must confront. I have been most impressed with the many superbly qualified oncologists I have met—men and women who have been trained in some of the best centers in this country and abroad. I have lectured so far on six of the world's seven continents. That leaves Antarctica, and if anyone establishes a medical school or cancer center there, I'm ready to go!

13

No Longer a Dream:
Eliminating Cancer in *My* Lifetime

We were sitting at a long, oval table in Conference Room 10, Building 31C at the National Institutes of Health just outside Washington, D.C., for one of those formulaic meetings that require my presence on a fairly regular basis. This one was the 125th meeting of the National Cancer Advisory Board on February 11, 2003, and my colleagues and I, most of whom had known each other for years, were listening to one of our own speak: Dr. Andrew von Eschenbach, director of the National Cancer Institute.

Dr. von Eschenbach was marking the end of his first year at the head of NCI, the government's main channel for funneling about $5 billion a year into cancer research and education, and he chose that moment to drop a bombshell. Using a term familiar to those of us who had worked at the American Cancer Society, Dr. von Eschenbach explained that NCI was setting a "challenge goal" to shape the mission and vision of the institute for the future. That goal, he said, was "to eliminate the suffering and death due to cancer and to do it by 2015."

Eliminate? Not cut, not reduce, but eliminate! By 2015? A mere twelve years? I wondered if I had heard my colleague correctly. How could he say that? There were seventeen of us sitting at the table listening to von Eschenbach, and several of us glanced around the room to gauge the reaction of our fellow members.

I noticed lots of raised eyebrows and quizzical expressions. Certainly health professionals had made great progress against the disease. We had learned vast amounts about the behavior of cancer cells and the causes of cancer. We had invented new surgical approaches and made breakthroughs in chemotherapy and radiation. We had taught generations to look for and recognize signs of cancer, to take the new tests we had devised, and to catch the disease earlier than ever. But the mere word "cancer" still casts a terrifying shadow over patients, their families, and even among the growing number of survivors. "The big C," they call it. And Andy was saying, from his bully pulpit at the helm of the greatest source of cancer funding in the world, that he intended to eliminate "suffering and death due to cancer" in a dozen short years.

My first thought was, "You can't be serious, Andy." Perhaps I had missed a qualifier. No, he repeated his challenge.

During the coffee break, some of my colleagues just shook their heads. We all knew Andy. He had been a distinguished cancer surgeon at M. D. Anderson in Houston for years, had helped launch the National Dialogue on Cancer (now C-Change). He had been president-elect of the American Cancer Society before being appointed at NCI. Say what you will about his challenge goal, we concluded that he was not speaking from ignorance. His statement represented a giant leap in thinking about cancer mortality, though. Only three years earlier the American Cancer Society—with Andy on its board—set a similarly lofty goal to cut cancer deaths in half by 2015. And that was seen as ambitious at the time.

Von Eschenbach's remarks touched off a lively discussion in

the community of cancer specialists and lay advocates. It was such a tempting thought—an amazing concept, really. He had not said we would eliminate cancer itself, but eliminate suffering and death from cancer. This meant that we would have to learn how to manage cancer as a chronic disease, the same way we manage high blood pressure or diabetes.

It's a laudable goal, certainly, and as I thought about it and discussed it with Andy and with other colleagues during the months that followed, I began to come around. I see Andy regularly. He is vice chair, and I am chair of the board of C-Change, and we have worked together at the American Cancer Society as well as on the National Cancer Advisory Board. He has stuck to his guns and doesn't hesitate to press his case for the target he set.

I am a clinician and a teacher, not a laboratory researcher. And as one frequently called on for advice and guidance, I have tried to follow the research, watch the trends and be ready to change my recommendations when the findings justify change. I am constantly updating my techniques and lectures to keep pace with the state of my practice, trying never to get stuck in a comfortable rut on familiar ground. Certainly tremendous progress has been made since I first went into medicine. Technological advances, such as mammograms, colonoscopies, and PET scans have afforded great breakthroughs in early detection. New drugs to attack cancer cells are coming out all the time. New devices and techniques enable us surgeons to get at cancerous tissue we couldn't reach before and to be much more precise about what we do remove and what we don't.

When von Eschenbach issued his challenge I thought about the impact of modern sciences such as genomics and proteomics, the development of therapies targeting specific cells in the body, and the implementation of nanotechnologies that use single atoms and molecules to build electronic circuits and devices. I realized that von Eschenbach's goal was at least plausible. I can't be certain we will make his deadline, but I no longer think it's an impossible dream. We have the infrastructure in place. We're making dramatic progress, and I am hopeful as never before.

In the meantime—and even if von Eschenbach's goal is met—our nation and the world face many challenges, some of them brought on by our own success. In May 2002, President George W. Bush named me to head the President's Cancer Panel, a three-member group that monitors national cancer programs and reports directly to the President on progress and obstacles in the struggle to control the terrifying and costly disease. By custom, the panel has one clinical cancer specialist, one basic scientist, and one lay member with a special interest in the disease. Presently serving with me are Margaret Kripke, a leading cancer researcher at Houston's M. D. Anderson Center; and Lance Armstrong, a survivor of metastatic testicular cancer and seven-time winner of the Tour de France cycling championship. One of the first areas we focused on under my leadership was the fastest-growing area of cancer work: survivorship.

In 1971, the year President Richard Nixon signed the National Cancer Act, there were three million cancer survivors in the United States. Today, thanks in part to earlier detection and more effective treatments, there are ten million. To be sure, part of that gain is due to the nation's increasingly aging population—cancer is more common as people grow older. Nonetheless, there are ten million people who live with the knowledge that they have *had* the disease. And while that warrants celebration, it also brings a host of problems, some of which we did not foresee.

In hearings across the country in 2003, the President's Cancer Panel listened to survivors, their families, and their doctors describe what it's like living beyond cancer: the constant fear of recurrence, the stigma, the awful debts people incur to save themselves, and the lingering pain and aftereffects of powerful drugs and radical surgery. One of the three members of our panel,

Dr. Leffall addresses an American Cancer Society luncheon on Capitol Hill sponsored by Marvella Bayh, ACS board member and wife of Senator Birch Bayh, April 1978. left to right: Senator Edward Kennedy, Senator Jacob Javits, Dr. George Wu of the Peoples Republic of China, Marvella Bayh, and Congressman John Brademas.
Courtesy, Senator Evan Bayh

Leffall, as secretary of the American College of Surgeons, carrying that organization's Great Mace at its annual convocation ceremony, 1991.
Courtesy, Oscar & Associates, Inc.

College and med school roommate George Rawls (left) and Leffall reunite at Leffall's ACS presidential induction reception, 1995; pictured with Rawl's wife Lula (right) and the author's son Donney (second fr. Left).

Courtesy, Chuck Giorno Photography

Dr. and Mrs. Leffall at an American College of Surgeons dinner, 1995.

Courtesy, Chuck Giorno Photography © 1995

Dr. Leffall at the 1990 "Anatomy of Hate" Conference in Oslo, Norway, with co-panelists, Nobel laureates Elie Wiesel and Günter Grass.

Courtesy, Henry Grossman ©

Dr. Leffall meets President and Mrs. Ronald Reagan at a dinner honoring National Gallery of Art founder Andrew Mellon in 1983.

Courtesy, Rex Allen Stucky Photography

David Mahoney (left), CEO of The Dana Foundation, and board members William Safire (right) and Dr. Leffall chat after the Foundation's annual awards dinner, 1997.

Courtesy, The Dana Foundation

Dr. Leffall celebrates the 50th anniversary of the HUCM General Surgery Residency Program at the 1986 Drew-Syphax Lecture. Left to right: Leffall; Dr. Dean Warren, President-elect, American College of Surgeons; his wife Eileen; lecturer Dr. Claude H. Organ Jr., professor of surgery at the University of Oklahoma; and Dr. Burke Syphax.

Courtesy, Howard University College of Medicine

Dr. Leffall and fourth-generation cancer survivor Zora Kramer Brown at the fifteenth anniversary gala of the Breast Cancer Resource Committee, an organization she founded to focus on the special needs of African American women.

Courtesy, Jason Miccolo Johnson © 2004

Dr. Leffall, board Chairman of the Susan G. Komen Breast Cancer Foundation, with that organization's founder, Nancy Brinker.

Courtesy, Lynn Hornor Keith

Dr. Leffall with Lane Adams, American Cancer Society Executive Vice President, during his term as President. Adams was a chief supporter of the 1979 ACS conference on African Americans and cancer.

Courtesy, American Cancer Society

The author in Kennebunkport, Maine, in 1998 with founding members of the National Dialogue on Cancer (now C-Change). Left to right: Harmon Eyre of the American Cancer Society; his wife Julie; Carole Seffrin, wife of American Cancer Society CEO John Seffrin; Former First Lady Barbara Bush; Dr. Leffall; Former President George H. W. Bush; John Seffrin (back row); and Andrew von Eschenbach, director of the National Cancer Institute.

Courtesy, American Cancer Society

Dr. Leffall with Senator Dianne Feinstein (D-CA), vice chair of C-Change.

Courtesy, Senator Dianne Feinstein

Dr. Leffall with fellow member of the President's Cancer Panel, cyclist Lance Armstrong, at a press conference in Paris, July 2003. Armstrong, a cancer survivor, had just won his fifth Tour de France.

Courtesy, Jonathan Devich/epicimages.us

Dr. Leffall with Dr. Wayne B. Tuckson, founder of the HUCM LaSalle D. Leffall Jr. Surgical Society.

Courtesy, Howard University College of Medicine

Dr. Leffall with one of his many successful students, Dr. Edward E. Cornwell III, Professor and Chief of the Adult Trauma Center at Johns Hopkins University Hospital and past President of the Society of Black Academic Surgeons.

Courtesy, Chuck Giorno Photography

In 1992, Dr. Leffall was named the first HUCM Charles R. Drew Professor of Surgery. Shown here at a ceremony honoring him with (fr. left to right) Harvard University's Churchill Professor of Surgery Dr. Gerald Austen; HUCM Dean Charles H. Epps; and District of Columbia Mayor Sharon Pratt Kelly.

Courtesy, Howard University College of Medicine

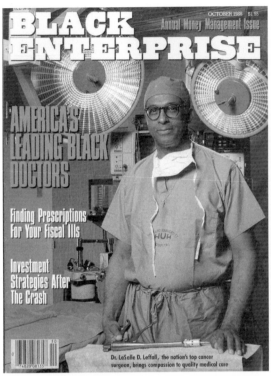

Dr. Leffall first graced the cover of *Black Enterprise* magazine for its October 1988 issue. He was also featured on *BE*'s August 2001 cover.

Courtesy, Jeffrey Henson Scales

Dr. Leffall in academic regalia as President of the American College of Surgeons, 1996.

Reprinted with permission, American College of Surgeons, Chicago, IL

Dr. Leffall receives an honorary fellowship award in 2004 from Sir Peter Morris, President of the Royal College of Surgeons of England, in London.

Courtesy, Ede & Ravenscroft

Dr. Leffall standing beside a portrait of himself commissioned for the HUCM "Wall of Deans" by the Class of 1970.

Courtesy, Howard University College of Medicine

In 1989, Dr. Leffall returned to his hometown of Quincy, Florida, to attend a ceremony naming a surgical wing of the local Gadsden Memorial Hospital in his honor.

Courtesy, James D. Brown Jr.

Dr. Leffall reached another important milestone during that same trip to Florida when he visited a street renamed in his honor: "Dr. LaSalle Leffall Drive."

Courtesy, James D. Brown Jr.

Lance Armstrong, is among the most famous survivors in the world, having found a successful treatment for his testicular cancer. He is as sensitive as anyone I have seen to the possibilities—and the practical problems—of survivorship.

On the day before the race ended, Lance was leading by seconds in his fifth consecutive Tour de France when I boarded a plane to be in Paris when he crossed the finish line. The President's Cancer Panel had convened a conference in Lisbon earlier in the year with a group of European survivors to look at the different ways other countries handle the problems associated with survivorship. We reassembled many of the participants for a press conference at the end of the race to focus attention on the great promise of surviving cancer. We figured that even if Armstrong came in second we would have a great event, but we needn't have worried. I was standing in the throng of thousands in the Champs Élysées when Lance won the race by a mere fifty-five seconds.

It was an exciting and amazing accomplishment. Everyone was screaming, and I'm sure I was yelling at least as loud as anyone there in the tumult of the race's end. Lance stopped off somewhere to thank his teammates, then made his way back to the hotel where we were to hold our press conference. As the two of us walked into the room, where dozens of television cameras were focused on us and where reporters from the world were waiting, Armstrong leaned over and, nodding toward the other survivors we had assembled, whispered in my ear: "Remember, this is not about me; it's about them."

That was typical of the man the French call "*un grand Monsieur*"—a class act.

Lance joined me and Margaret Kripke at other meetings around the United States that year to learn from other survivors. As we listened to the testimony of young people, adults in their middle years, and the elderly, I realized that in our determined efforts to save lives now, we physicians and surgeons still often overlook what lies ahead for our patients. For example, Karen Dyer, a twenty-four-year-old woman diagnosed with cancer of the skeletal muscles when she was fifteen, told us her chemotherapy has caused early menopause that requires hormone therapy, which carries its own risks and uncertainties. She has since evolved, she claimed, from constant fear of a recurrence of her disease to fear of the longer-term effects of her splenectomy operation and of possible problems related to osteoporosis, sexuality, and cardiac problems. And yes, she stated, "even wrinkles." Ms. Dyer recently began working with a new organization dedicated to helping cancer patients who face infertility.

Her concern is a real one and one that needs to be addressed. Before surgical techniques were refined to the point we surgeons could leave intact much of the tissue we previously removed, and before we had a range of drugs available for chemotherapy or could wield radiation with needlepoint accuracy, our patients didn't have many options. We had to deal with the most immediate issue facing us: cutting out the cancer. Today we can sometimes shield the reproductive organs before treatment or capture sperm or eggs for preservation if those organs must be removed or damaged by radiation. Parenthood is thus no longer an impossible dream for cancer survivors today.

We also heard from Angie Farfan, who was diagnosed with cancer at ages four, ten, and fourteen. She told us that at age thirty, she requires so much specialized attention that she is often overwhelmed and confused: "I am followed by a pulmonologist, a cardiologist, a gynecologist, a prosthetist, and an oncologist; for every 'ist' there is, I have one," she said. "I coordinate all that care by myself. . . . I have to reeducate everybody on my issues, and it's almost like they don't believe me; I have to convince them."

Older survivors also have their own set of problems, ranging from fulfilling their needs for intimacy to addressing concerns about body image and the sudden dependence on others just to get around, fix meals, or go to the doctor. The health insurance problems of survivors alone are daunting and often financially crippling and heartbreaking for them and their families. We heard many stories about the depression, despair, and the family collapse that sometimes follows on the heels of supposedly successful initial treatment of cancer.

"All of the times that I went for the various examinations I always was alone," shared Grace Butler, a sixty-seven-year-old survivor of colorectal cancer. "I remember sitting one day waiting for the dye to go through my system, and I am looking at everybody coming and going. Everybody had somebody, and there I sat. I couldn't help it. I wept. I had nobody."[4]

Our panel concluded that life after cancer is often a poorly charted journey, and we recommended reforms in treatment and follow-up, record keeping, counseling, fertility options and health insurance coverage. From individual steps that doctors can take to comprehensive reform of the nation's health care system, we set down a series of steps that should be taken by health care workers, lawmakers, schools, and advocacy groups to increase sensitivity to the special needs of cancer survivors and ensure that they receive the follow-up care they often don't get today.

In 2004, the panel launched a review of whether the vast sums spent on cancer research have translated into improved outcomes for cancer patients. My approach has been to ask a simple question: We spend all this money; what good does it do?

We have looked at the vital role that clinical trials play in getting the most advanced treatments to patients diagnosed with cancer. We have also considered recommendations that promising experimental therapies be offered as first-line treatments, rather than as a last resort when conventional efforts have failed and the cancer has advanced. Lance has been one of the strongest advocates for wider participation in clinical trials. His own cancer was treated using drugs that were no longer

---

[4] Cases cited are from the public records of the President's Cancer Panel.

experimental, but he credits his survival to those who participated in trials and provided the knowledge needed to help him.

I must point out that Lance probably has the most determined and most positive attitude of anyone I have ever known.
If all patients approached their cancers with his absolute conviction that they could beat it, von Eschenbach's goal would be easier to reach.

Lance's cancer began in one testicle, and by the time it was
discovered when he was twenty-five years old, it had already
spread to his lungs and brain. He underwent two operations in
late 1996, one for removal of the cancerous testicle and the
other to remove two lesions from his brain. He then had four
rounds of chemotherapy using a combination of powerful tumor-
destroying drugs to kill the remaining cancer cells in his body.

The results, of course, are the stuff of legend. Lance got back
on his racing bike and proved himself to be the best bicyclist in
the world.

Even before the outcome of his treatment was known, Lance
established the Lance Armstrong Foundation to help other cancer patients and encourage them to face their illness with his
motto: "Live strong." I'm sure it was not only his success as a
survivor but his commitment to helping others like himself that
led to his appointment to the President's Cancer Panel.

In addition to examining the place of clinical trials in cancer
treatment, the panel has looked at legal barriers intended to pro-
tect patient privacy that actually inhibit collaborative research.
We contend that scientists with different strengths and specialties should work together to develop new treatments, but they
may be hindered by concerns about sharing patient information.
The right of every patient to privacy must be respected, but at
the same time we believe that researchers should have access to
the information they need to team up in the search for the cure.

We also heard testimony that the large population of unin-
sured, underserved, and working poor in this country doesn't
have access to cutting-edge therapies. That's wrong, and I

strongly believe our panel must and should offer recommendations to correct it. Our panel's third member, Margaret Kripke, Ph.D., an immunologist and executive vice president at the University of Texas's M. D. Anderson Cancer Center, has helped guide us through the research labyrinth to better understand what happens to the work that gets done in the laboratory and whether it gets properly communicated to those who can use it to save lives.

With all the progress we have made in cancer treatment and research during my long career, I still remind myself every single day that my primary responsibility is to help every patient I see, to tell her or him the truth—with sensitivity and compassion—and to always hold out hope for success while never giving misleading or evasive answers to fundamental questions. When you give people hope, I believe, you grant them one of the greatest of all human joys: the joy of anticipation. Perhaps then will they think that there is *something* that can be done to help them. Maybe then they can believe that they too have a chance. Together, we can *beat* this!

That said, I never force bad news on patients who don't want to hear it. I also try never to be crass or too blunt. I consciously try to speak with my patients in an unhurried pace, repeating myself often and trying to help them understand their medical situations and all their options.

Some patients deny they have cancer, insisting that there's been a mistake. They may lash out at me or at other doctors. I don't try to force such people to accept their diagnosis; I just continue to do everything I can to treat what they have and still answer their questions honestly. I don't believe in hiding the truth, but I don't try to force it on a patient if he or she doesn't want to accept what I know.

I have seen many patients, in their desperation, grasp for unproven methods of treatment. For example, a man with advanced colon cancer that had spread to his liver told me he had heard that shark cartilage might cure him. We had already tried standard chemotherapy, but those drugs had not succeeded in slowing the course of his disease. I told him I had heard about shark cartilage treatments but was not aware of any data that indicated it was of real value. He went somewhere and got it anyway, but that too failed to affect his cancer. He was dead within months.

In an even more heartbreaking case, a patient of mine with advanced breast cancer told me she had heard about a hyperthermia treatment being given in upstate New York that offered a cure for her cancer. She acknowledged that it was very expensive, but she planned to mortgage her home to finance the therapy.

"If I'm not alive, I won't be around to use the money anyway," she said.

Hyperthermia, also called thermal therapy, uses heat, usually applied locally to tumors, in an attempt to kill cancer cells. A number of studies have shown that when combined with radiation or chemotherapy, hyperthermia treatment may reduce the size of some tumors. I told her, however, that I didn't think it had been shown to help people with advanced breast cancers like hers.

"Well, *you're* not doing anything for me!" she said emphatically. I was taken aback because I was treating her pain effectively and helping her get proper nutrition. "I *still* have the cancer!"

She was correct that I had been unable to cure her; we had found her cancer too late. She soon took out a new mortgage on her home and underwent four of the expensive treatments. They did her no good, and she died about six months later.

I understand that people cling to unproven methods—even cruel hoaxes—when they believe no good alternatives are available to them. In such cases, I always try to explain the role of science—of clinical trials and medicine—which is based on evidence, not conjecture or mere tradition. To me, that is the only ethical course. But if a patient comes upon something that does not interfere with that science, such as adopting a macrobiotic diet or taking high doses of particular vitamins, I try to be supportive. I stress that they should not forsake proven methods for unproven ones, but I try not to dash their hopes if they have confidence in alternative approaches.

I don't hesitate to tell patients who question my approach that the NIH has a National Center for Complementary and Alternative Medicine that studies a variety of approaches to treatment, ranging from traditional Chinese medicine to spiritual techniques that use prayer, the laying on of hands, and mind–body interventions to help people get better. I don't suggest that there is any proof that such methods can cure cancer, but neither do I discourage anyone from exploring avenues they believe can help them.

In my line of work, of course, I don't win every time. Cancer earned its awful reputation because it not only kills but also sometimes takes its dreadful toll slowly, returning when least expected, sapping a person's strength and hope, and inflicting deep, sometimes intractable pain. Such circumstances challenge the resolve and ethics of any doctor whose job is to comfort and heal. I know some sincere doctors and patients who recommend euthanasia in terminal cases and who support thoughtful life-ending decisions with stringent safeguards, such as those mandated recently in Oregon. But I was taught to preserve life, and I personally cannot bring myself to help a patient die by providing the means to kill them.

I once was treating a young man who had developed cancer of the rectum and had ignored persistent rectal bleeding because he thought it was due to hemorrhoids. As his disease advanced, the cancer invaded the nerves in his pelvis, causing unrelenting pain. The patient, in his late thirties, pleaded with me to give him something so he could die.

I explained that I could not, and would not, carry out his wish and that I was taught to preserve life and not take it. I persuaded him to try a morphine pump that could be implanted beneath the skin of his abdomen with a catheter that led into his spinal canal to deliver a constant dose of the powerful drug. That approach gave the young man immediate, dramatic relief; and although I couldn't stop the spread of his cancer, he was able to go home, continue to work, and spend precious time pain-free with his family. He survived for nearly a year after that, and before he succumbed, he thanked me for not giving in to his desperate plea. He treasured the extra time he got to spend at home with his two young children without the misery of that awful, driving pain.

Others have asked for similar release, and I have wrestled with their requests knowing full well the depth of their suffering. But I don't believe that we physicians should give ourselves the ultimate power to decide who should live and who should die. We know that many patients reach the point that they want us to. They sometimes seem in such misery that I really do wish I could do their bidding, but for that, I believe I must always try instead to alleviate their pain. We have made great advances in pain management, and I for one do not hesitate to use them. In severe cases I don't worry about the implications of administering addictive drugs. In the late stages of cancer, that point becomes irrelevant anyway. I do not, however, believe doctors must use all of the means at our disposal to keep someone alive when the quality of that person's life has lost its meaning.

As in the case of my own mother, I know that there is a time when even our most intensive cancer treatment does not make our patients better—even if it prolongs vital functions. The ethical issues surrounding cancer have grown more complex with our increased knowledge of how to save—or at least preserve—life. I, however, fall back on the tenets I was taught, not only as a medical student but also as a young boy raised by loving parents in a small Florida town where I learned that helping others was a virtue and hurting them was just plain wrong.

Surgeons don't always have the luxury of time when making ethical decisions. As noted medical ethicist Edmund Pellegrino puts it, we must often make concrete judgments in situations where action must be taken despite the uncertainty of the immediate situation. It is at such moments that we physicians turn to what he called that "one irreducible foundation of all clinical medicine—the relationship between the one who is ill and the one who professes to help and heal." That is also when we need to demonstrate equanimity under duress. The final criterion of whether a decision we make is morally sound is whether it is made for the good of the patient.[5] I often see patients who veer from self-pity to mordant bravado in their efforts to muster the courage to confront a bewildering illness. As surgeons, we must have the strength to make for them the hard ethical decisions they may not be able to make for themselves.

Years ago, after reading and rereading Leo Tolstoy's *The Death of Ivan Ilyich*, I wrote that the lesson of Ivan Ilyich was that by lying to him about his illness, his wife and his physicians only made his pain worse. Although not diagnosed as such, Ilyich probably had cancer. As Tolstoy put it, his character

> ". . . suffered most of all from the lie, the lie which, for some reason, everyone accepted: that he was not dying but was simply ill, and that if he stayed calm and underwent treatment he could expect good results. Yet he knew that regardless of what was done, all he could expect was more agonizing suffering and death. And he was tortured by this lie, tortured by the fact that they refused to acknowledge what he and everyone else knew, that they wanted to lie about his horrible condition and to force him to become a party to that lie. This lie, a lie perpetrated on the eve of his death, a lie that was bound

---

[5] Edmund D. Pellegrino, M.D., "The Common Devotion—Cushing's Legacy and Medical Ethics Today." *Journal of Neurosurgery, 59*: 567–573, 1983.

to degrade the awesome, solemn act of his dying to the level of their social calls, their draperies, and the sturgeon they ate for dinner, was an excruciating torture for Ivan Ilyich."

Ilyich, I believe, would have had a more dignified death had he been treated with honesty and compassion. Too often we doctors regard patients in their terminal phases of life not as though they are dying, but as if they are already dead. We often hear about death with dignity, but we must realize that we are really talking about preserving our patients' dignity while they are still alive.

Young surgeons, I once told an audience of the American College of Surgeons, are often motivated by the exuberance of inexperience and the romance of the novice, but with time they learn reasoned thought and judgment. What I also try to instill in them is that they must learn to relate directly to their patients. It is easy to rely on charts and tests and small talk, and we can always call in another magical machine. But no matter how good our technology gets, we must always keep our patients in mind as the objects of our affection and remember to always exercise good judgment on their behalf. If we do that honestly, openly, and with compassion, we will be acting ethically and need not fear the outcome.

14

Grace Notes

When my college classmate Cannonball Adderley came to Washington and we got together, he loved to expound on the intricacies of harmony, melody, rhythm, and counterpoint, and I loved to share with him the latest advances in surgical techniques and oncology. To my delight, he was just as interested in my work as I was in hearing about some up-and-coming musical genius or a new song he was working on. It was during one such session listening to jazz in my den that he taught me about the meaning of grace notes, and I've been alert for them ever since, not only in music, but in my life.

As "Cannon" put it, a grace note's timing doesn't affect the rhythm of the bar, it's just "something a little extra, like an ornament."

The day after I learned what he meant by this term, I tried it out on a patient of mine. I had operated on that woman for cancer earlier and she came to see me for a follow-up exam. She said she was looking for someone else to drive her to her regular radiation treatments. When I asked why, she explained that the person who had been giving her a ride just didn't want to do it anymore. I asked how she knew, and she replied, "I just *know*." It was not a medical matter, of course, but the woman was my patient, and I wanted her to feel as comfortable as possible about her treatments so I pursued the issue.

"I know that it's easy to tell when someone's doing something for you because he or she really wants to or if they're doing something out of obligation," I told her. "It's hard to fake sincerity." Then I added Cannonball's wisdom: "Music can be quite lovely without the grace notes, but it becomes something special with them."

She looked at me oddly, wondering what I meant as I stumbled around in my head, trying to frame my thoughts while I was talking. "You see," I continued, "you're getting your radiation treatment, but you're missing that special human treatment. And it doesn't matter whether the person who's helping you is a volunteer or a practicing physician or a surgeon, caregivers should always find a way to give that something extra—that *grace note*—to let you know they are not just performing a duty, but that they really care . . ."

My voice must have trailed off, but I think I had captured appropriately what Cannonball meant—and what it meant for me as a physician.

Grace notes, I realized, are those feelings and actions that represent a genuine sensitivity and compassion for those in one's care. My patient sat across from me, smiling and nodding in approval. She understood, too. She seemed satisfied that I had listened to her. She decided to continue her usual transportation for her treatments.

Many of my personal grace notes have been learning experiences, not necessarily beautiful at the time, but humbling and lasting lessons that I pass along to my students. For example, when I was a first-year resident at Freedmen's Hospital and somewhat impressed with my importance, the chief resident once assigned me to perform an axillary lymph node biopsy or, in laymen's terms, to take a sample of lymphatic tissue from a patient's armpit. This is normally a minor procedure, and I was a bit annoyed that he didn't give me a more challenging case. Having no choice, however, I reluctantly accepted the assignment.

I quickly discovered in the OR that I couldn't even *find* that patient's axillary lymph node! It seemed to be hidden somewhere, perhaps behind some major blood vessels and nerves going to the arm. I searched for nearly an hour, in growing embarrassment, before finally concluding that I had to call the chief resident for help. He arrived within minutes and, with no sign of rancor or dismay, swiftly and skillfully located the elusive node, excised it, and left me to close the wound.

That experience taught me there are no minor procedures, just minor surgeons. I resolved not to be one of them.

The next year, while I was a second-year surgical resident on the Georgetown Service at Gallinger Municipal Hospital (later D.C. General), a young black woman came into the emergency room late one night complaining of severe abdominal pain and nausea. Dead tired after being on duty for forty-eight hours—and on my feet for what seemed like forty-seven of those—I asked the woman what I thought were the appropriate questions to ask about her condition. I ruled out some of the more obvious possibilities and made a tentative diagnosis of acute pancreatitis. I ordered lab tests of her serum amylase levels, expecting those to confirm my finding.

The results, however, came back negative. The levels were normal, indicating my diagnosis was probably wrong. I ordered some more blood tests, which showed that her hemoglobin and hematocrit levels were quite low. Something was wrong, but it was probably not with her pancreas.

I was perplexed, but as I thought about her symptoms and the test results, it occurred to me that she could be experiencing a sickle-cell anemia crisis. Sickle cell anemia, an uncommon hereditary disorder that strikes people of African descent as well as some Middle Eastern and Hispanic populations, results in the formation of red blood cells that are shaped like a sickle instead of the donut shape of a normal cell. The sickle-shaped blood cells tend to be stiff and sticky and clump together, causing painful blockages in small blood vessels, particularly in the abdominal area. The result can be excruciatingly painful.

I returned to my patient and asked her if by chance she had sickle cell anemia.

"Yes," she replied matter-of-factly.

"Why didn't you say so?" I asked, exasperation showing in my voice.

"You didn't ask me," she said.

It seems simple enough, but physicians frequently need to be reminded that their patients know more about themselves than their doctors do—at least during the initial clinical exam. Patients may not be aware, however, about what information is relevant or what their doctors need to know. And if the physician doesn't ask, it can take a long time to track down the source of a problem.

We doctors sometimes forget about our patients in other ways, too. As a young attending surgeon, I was conducting ward rounds one morning with a group of visiting surgeons and the hospital house staff. We reached the bed of a male patient with non-operable esophageal cancer who had just had a feeding tube placed through the abdominal wall into his stomach because he was no longer able to swallow his food. My colleagues gathered around me at the foot of the patient's bed, listening intently to my observations and asking probing questions about the case. The patient sat upright the whole time, squirming uncomfortably, his bare legs dangling off the side of the bed. He shifted his attention from physician to physician while I extolled the virtues of tube feeding as a means of providing nutritional support in cases such as his.

Just as our band of experts was about to move on, the patient grabbed my arm and pleaded, "Doc, can you wait a minute? I'm getting ready to have my breakfast." I instinctively glanced at my watch but asked the group to wait. Then, with great fanfare and deliberation, the patient took the open end of the feeding tube in one hand and held it up for all to see. With his other hand, he slowly, carefully poured the gastrostomy solution into the tube. I soon grew impatient with the demonstration because the patient was delaying my morning rounds and whispered to the chief resident that he should say something to the man because we had to move on. The chief resident, however, said nothing as the exhibition continued until the last drop of solution had dripped into the tube.

The patient then turned to me with a devilish grin on his face and said, "Thanks for waiting, Doc. That was delicious!"

I finally got it.

With all my talk about how medical science had developed such wonderful techniques to improve patient nutrition, I had forgotten that this man could no longer eat or enjoy a meal.

I may have been the teacher, but he was doing the teaching.

One brutally cold, snowy afternoon in Washington, I was the attending surgeon covering the surgical clinic at the hospital when a grandmother from Anacostia, one of the least privileged neighborhoods in the nation's capital, arrived late for an appointment to have her sutures removed after a major abdominal operation. It was 3:05, and the clinic hours were from 1:00 to 3:00. The surgical resident, noting the time, told her the clinic was closed and refused to see her. When the elderly patient began to cry, right there in the middle of the waiting room, the nurse on duty called me. I told her I'd be right down.

The resident, overhearing the nurse's conversation and learning that I was coming to the clinic myself, immediately indicated that he would see the patient after all and told the nurse to tell me I didn't need to bother. I sent word through her that he was not to examine the woman until I arrived and that we would see her together.

When I got to the waiting room, I introduced myself to the woman as the attending physician in charge and apologized to her on behalf of the hospital, clinic, and staff. I invited her into the evaluation room, and she explained that she had set out for the clinic shortly after noon but had been slowed down by a terrible traffic snarl caused by the snow. I removed her stitches, spoke to her about her recovery since the operation, and sent her relieved on her way home.

Afterward I asked the resident to walk with me back to my office. On the way, he nervously explained that had he known how important it was to me that this patient be seen he would have treated her, despite her tardiness and the harsh weather conditions that were threatening to make our own trips home extremely difficult. I listened quietly to his litany of excuses, and when we reached the privacy of my office I told him that he had missed the point entirely.

"If you'd learned that your own grandmother—or any family member for that matter—had received the treatment or nontreatment that you gave that patient today, you'd be ready for mortal combat," I said. "Today you had the opportunity to show a patient what a true physician is, and you came up short. You should never be found wanting, especially when it comes to patient care."

"But sir, I'm not really like that," he insisted. "I'm a *caring* doctor!"

"Well today you had the chance to show that, and you failed," I told him, pulling no punches. "You'd better make up your mind quickly if this is the profession for you, young man, because the kind of behavior you demonstrated today violates every code of ethical conduct that physicians and surgeons hold dear."

Tears streamed down the young resident's cheeks, first slowly, then in a steady flow. He promised me that what had

Notes

happened would never happen again. I believe he was sincere and have kept an eye on his career. He completed his residency, passed the American Board of Surgery examination on his first attempt and moved to the South, where he now has a successful surgical practice.

Numerous studies have shown that, as a group, we physicians are woefully inadequate in our treatment of the pain that so often accompanies a serious condition like cancer. Even worse, many doctors don't even acknowledge the pain their patients suffer and the impact of that pain on the quality of their lives. I have seen too many patients in the advanced stages of cancer, their bodies wracked by excruciating, nearly constant pain. Most young and relatively inexperienced staff physicians typically avoid prescribing strong pain medication for such patients because they don't want their patients to become addicted to drugs. Over the years I have come to believe it is one of the primary duties of cancer physicians to relieve that pain. If addiction becomes an issue, which it rarely does, we can deal with it if and when we have to.

Physicians' insensitivity to their patients' pain is not just a matter for end-stage cancer and addictive drugs, however. I remember once explaining to a patient that I was going to perform a procedure under local anesthesia. He asked if it would hurt.

"You'll have a little discomfort, that's all," I told him.

The patient looked at me—hard—for what must have been a good ten seconds, then asked me slowly, as if communicating with a resistant child, "Tell me, doctor. How does 'a little discomfort' differ from pain?"

Pain is relative. As physicians, and especially surgeons, we must learn never to trivialize our patients' pain. It is real and an important aspect of treatment and healing. We are much better at easing pain now than we used to be, however, and we ought to be constantly on the alert for how to use our knowledge to make our patients comfortable if we can.

One patient once complained to me that she was "just *hurtin'*" and that the residents in the hospital weren't giving her enough pain medication. "Jus' what kind of doctors are they, anyway?" she asked. "They can't even relieve *pain!*"

Early in my career, I had a breast cancer patient who had been referred to me by her brother-in-law, a senior physician who had been one of my professors in medical school. The patient kept insisting that she didn't have cancer, that at best I had misdiagnosed her and at worst I was fabricating the whole story about her disease. With rising frustration I gently but consistently informed her that she did indeed have cancer and that it had spread to the lymph nodes in her armpit. I tried to persuade her to agree to an operation—and soon—if she was to have any chance of surviving the disease. Still, she resisted for several weeks, stubbornly refusing to even discuss the matter with her brother-in-law the doctor or with other members of her family. Finally, they persuaded her to proceed, although she refused to acknowledge why she was having surgery.

While she was recuperating, my former professor called me to ask how I thought his sister-in-law was doing. I told him the same thing I had told her: that the operation went well. Then he stopped me in my tracks.

"Leffall, I've got to tell you this," he began. "I know my sister-in-law hasn't been the easiest patient, but she told me the reason why she always gives you such a hard time. She said it's because you always give her bad news."

My jaw must have dropped. "I don't understand! The woman has cancer! What else could I have told her? I've tried to give her the best care possible."

"I know, I know," he said, trying to calm me before going on. "I believe that a patient should be told the truth and kept informed. But remember, patients need some victories, too!"

My old professor was handing me the keys to how I should talk to the thousands of patients I would see during my career who were facing a serious, perhaps even terminal, struggle with cancer. I learned then to tell my patients not only the truth, which is a tenet of faith with me, but to give them something to hope for as well. Instead of telling the woman in denial that she should face reality, I could have told her that we had found a tumor in her breast but that there was no evidence it had spread to her lungs, bones, or other vital organs. I could have said, "We can stop it, but we have to act quickly." There is hope in those statements. When patients have hope, I learned, they have a reason to keep living.

I sincerely believe in the science of medicine. I have devoted my entire professional life to it. But there is a spiritual side to all of us that transcends that science and sometimes produces results science alone cannot. My personal faith tells me this, and I have watched it manifest in my practice.

I believe that the more I have learned about medicine, the more spiritual my outlook about health and disease has become. I have watched many patients make surprising progress that can't be explained medically, and I believe that spirituality gives people hope when the best earthly efforts seem to be failing.

Prayer has been a source of comfort and strength to me since childhood.

I was making oncology rounds one day on the gynecology service with some colleagues when I was still a resident, and the professor conducting the rounds gathered us together in the room of a woman who had been diagnosed with choriocarcinoma, a highly malignant tumor of the uterus. With his back to the patient, the professor stood facing our group of physicians-in-training. Poker-faced, he dispassionately reviewed the particulars of the woman's case, and in a hushed but audible voice he noted that she could be expected to live only six to nine months. The patient said nothing to the doctor or to anyone else while we were in the room, but later I came upon her on the ward floor, staring out the window. She called over to me and told me she'd heard what the professor had told us.

"Can you believe that, Dr. Leffall?" she asked. "It's like I'm just some kind of case study, not a person. Please don't you be like that when you get to be a *real* doctor."

A few months later, doctors at the National Cancer Institute discovered that a drug called methotrexate was highly effective in the treatment of choriocarcinoma, with cure rates approaching 90 percent. The patient was given the drug and was cured of her malignant tumor. Ironically, the doctor who had predicted her demise died within six months, and the patient lived a long, full life.

Her experience has helped teach me how to answer one of the most frequent questions I am asked by patients with cancer: "Doctor, what are my chances?"

We have many miracle drugs and advanced procedures that enable us to cure or at least extend the lives of patients who had virtually no chance of survival when I began my specialty. I can now be more optimistic in answering that question than ever before but, of course, I still see cases some might regard as hopeless, and I am bound by honor to tell the truth.

"With our current knowledge, we cannot cure you," I admit to the patient in those cases, "but I'm sure we can *help* you. And who knows? During the period of your treatment, some researcher, working somewhere in the world, may develop the cure that works for you." Then I usually tell them the story of the woman whose indomitable spirit and the discovery of methotrexate just in time kept her alive beyond her physician's best guess.

I have received more than my share of life's wonderful bounties. To have the opportunity to pursue a profession you truly love is one of life's greatest joys. Medicine has allowed me to become a teacher, a healer, and an advocate. Excellence is an often elusive yet unwavering goal that is attainable through discipline and perseverance. As a teacher I have always emphasized that excellence in patient care must be the physician's top priority.

A medical education allows one to be active in one or more of four areas—clinical care, teaching, administration, and research. I believe that I've had the best the profession can offer because I've been involved in all four of those areas during my professional career, always with the view that the patient has the role of primacy. The creation of new knowledge and the expansion of old knowledge are to me the hallmarks of research. More researchers are urgently needed to find answers to some of medicine's lingering enigmas. While seeking better diagnostic and therapeutic measures, we must maintain our efforts in prevention.

As I reflect on my long career, my most satisfying moments have come from providing care to surgical patients, teaching medical students, and mentoring surgical residents. Being a part of efforts to improve patients' health and train surgeons for the future has brought me incalculable and enduring joy. Further reflection reminds me of how disappointment can serve as a tremendous stimulus for achievement. In my case, rejection has served as a positive force for me to continue my quest for excellence and to prove my worth. Notwithstanding, the support of family, friends, and colleagues has been invaluable. The cooperation I have received from my professional colleagues over the years has enabled me to serve at the highest levels of surgical and oncological organizations. The aid I have received throughout my career only reinforces my duty to help my younger colleagues in their professional pursuits.

International travel has been an integral part of my professional life, allowing me to establish and maintain rapport with colleagues in foreign countries. Exchanging and sharing relevant information emphasizes the global nature of medicine and international cooperation in a personal way.

To have had a role beyond that of teacher and clinician in the fight against cancer—one of our most feared diseases—has brought me special gratification. When I chaired the 1979

American Cancer Society conference on cancer health disparities, I could never have dreamed that, a quarter century later, this topic would be a major priority of the National Cancer Institute and practically all voluntary cancer organizations.

On an April weekend in 1989 I returned to Quincy, Florida, to be honored by the citizens of my hometown for my achievements as a surgeon, medical professor, chairman of the Department of Surgery at Howard University College of Medicine, and the first black president of the American Cancer Society. I was proud to have assisted in the initiation of early cancer detection programs for racial and ethnic minorities and the elimination of disparities in cancer care for all Americans. My Howard colleagues and I had labored long and hard to increase the number of black surgical academicians and researchers.

My mother was still living in Quincy then, and Ruthie did not attend so that Mother could more fully share the place of honor with me. The town really celebrated, beginning with a police-escorted limousine from the Tallahassee airport for Mother and me and a weekend-long round of ceremonies that included a lively jazz concert by my old friend Nat Adderley, the late Cannonball's brother. The town named a street, a path, and the surgical wing of the Gadsden Memorial Hospital in my honor. At a reception in the Quincy Garden Club, Julia Woodward, the daughter of the late Pat Munroe (the banker who put his Quincy customers in Coca-Cola stock), came over and gave me a big hug while saying, "You have no idea how *proud* we are of you!"

The next day I went to the town's new high school and, speaking to the student body, revealed how much I loved practicing medicine and how important I felt it was to develop cancer-prevention habits such as not smoking and eating healthy food. Of course, I recounted the advice I had been given by my father, who had been principal of an earlier school in my hometown: "With a good education and hard work," my father said, "combined with honesty and integrity, there are no boundaries."

At a standing-room-only testimonial banquet that night in the new Quincy National Guard Armory, my eighty-year-old mother was particularly radiant as I escorted her to the platform. I knew she felt the same warmth I did from my former classmates, teachers, and several hundred "homefolks" in the audience, both black and white. We listened to a battery of distinguished speakers who spoke of their pride in, respect for, and admiration of my accomplishments—glowing tributes every one. Then it was my turn to speak.

I had given hundreds of speeches and lectures by that time and been all over the world, but as I looked out at that crowd and thanked the people of Quincy for taking such good care of my mother throughout the years I was filled with emotion. I can only hope that I fully expressed the joy I was feeling that night.

The next day the local newspapers had headlines such as "Streets Named After Nation's Top Cancer Surgeon"; "Native Son Returns"; and "LaSalle D. Leffall, M.D., Gadsden County's Gift to the World." I was confident that I—and so many others like me—had come a long, long way since I swept out the white and colored waiting rooms in the local doctor's office and my friends and I were reduced to sitting in the balcony at the Shaw movie theater.

Perhaps there were indeed, I realized, no boundaries. My father was right.

APPENDIX

Offices and Honors

Professional and Civic Organization Leadership Positions:

- President, American Cancer Society, 1978–1979
- President, Society of Surgical Oncology, 1978–1979
- President, American College of Surgeons, Metropolitan Washington Chapter, 1978–1979
- President, Society of Surgical Chairmen, 1988–1990
- President, D.C. Division, American Cancer Society, 1974–1976
- President, Washington Academy of Surgery, 1981–1982
- President, American College of Surgeons, 1995–1996
- President, Society of Black Academic Surgeons, 1997–1998
- Vice President, Society for Surgery of the Alimentary Tract, 1989–1990
- Second Vice President, American Surgical Association, 1989–1990
- Chairman, Executive Committee, Board of Governors, United Way of America 1989–1992
- Chairman, Susan G. Komen Breast Cancer Foundation, 2002–present
- Chairman, President's Cancer Panel—2002–present
- Chairman, Steering Committee (now Board of Directors), National Dialogue on Cancer (now C-Change) 1998–present
- Civilian Aide-at-Large to the Secretary of the U.S. Army, 1979–1981
- Secretary, American College of Surgeons, 1983–1992

Member of the Board of the Following Organizations:

- National Cancer Advisory Board, 1980–1986
- American Board of Surgery, 1981–1987
- Center on Addiction and Substance Abuse at Columbia University, 1992–2001

- Board of Directors, Medical Education for South African Blacks, 1986–2000
- The Dana Foundation, 1998–present

First African-American President of the Following Organizations:

- American Cancer Society
- Society of Surgical Oncology
- Society of Surgical Chairmen
- Washington Academy of Surgery
- American College of Surgeons

Honorary Degrees:

- Georgetown University
- University of Maryland
- Florida A&M University
- Meharry Medical College
- Clark University
- Morehouse School of Medicine
- Howard University
- Albany Medical College
- University of The South
- Amherst College
- Lafayette College
- Thomas Jefferson University

Honorary Fellowships:

- West African College of Surgeons, 1994
- International Society of Surgery, 1995
- College of Surgeons of South Africa, 1996
- Royal College of Physicians and Surgeons of Canada, 1996
- Deutsche Gesellschaft fuer Chirurgie (German Surgical Society), 1997
- American Society for Therapeutic Radiology and Oncology (honorable member), 2003
- Royal College of Surgeons of England, 2004

Other Awards:

- First prize, Charles R. Drew Fundamental Forum (resident competition) of the Surgical Section, National Medical Association, 1954

- Charles R. Drew Creative Services Medal (the highest honor given by the Charles R. Drew University of Medicine and Science), 1985
- Commander's Award for Public Service, Walter Reed Army Medical Center, 1995
- Distinguished Service Award, Surgical Section, National Medical Association, 1995
- Trumpet Award for Outstanding Achievement in Medicine, awarded by the Turner Broadcasting System, 1996
- Distinguished Professor of Surgery Award, Uniformed Services University of the Health Sciences, 1997.
- Heritage Award of the Society of Surgical Oncology (first awardee; to a past SSO president for significant contributions to oncology), 2001
- National Visionary Leadership Award, 2004

Honors Named for Dr. LaSalle D. Leffall Jr.:

- LaSalle D. Leffall Jr. Award, given by M. D. Anderson Hospital and the Intercultural Cancer Council of Houston, Texas, to persons who make outstanding contributions to cancer-control activities targeting socioeconomically disadvantaged populations; established in 1987.
- LaSalle D. Leffall Jr. Surgical Wing of the Gadsden Memorial Hospital in Quincy, Florida; dedicated in 1989.
- LaSalle D. Leffall Street and Path in Quincy, Florida; renamed in 1989.
- LaSalle D. Leffall Jr. Surgical Society, organized by former students and trainees of Dr. Leffall (convenes annually); established in 1994.
- LaSalle D. Leffall Jr. Endowed Chair in Surgery, Howard University College of Medicine; established in 1996.
- LaSalle D. Leffall Jr. Award, presented by the Washington, D.C.-Metropolitan Chapter of the American College of Surgeons to recognize surgeons' outstanding contributions to clinical care, research, teaching, and community activities; established in 1996.
- LaSalle D. Leffall Jr. Reading Room, Howard University Hospital, Department of Surgery; rededicated in 1995.
- LaSalle D. Leffall Jr. Prize, presented to a graduating senior Howard University College of Medicine student for outstanding performance in surgery; established in 1997.

- LaSalle D. Leffall Jr. Science Research Laboratory at Florida A&M University, Tallahassee, Florida; established in 1998.
- LaSalle D. Leffall Jr. Award for Best Attending in General Surgery, presented by the surgical residents of Howard University Hospital; established in 1999.

INDEX

197